"Shawn Carney and Steve Karlen have given us a clear, practical guide that walks readers through the current landscape in the pro-life versus pro-abortion debate and leaves them feeling confident in ending abortion."

— Lila Rose, President and Founder of Live Action

"Shawn Carney and Steve Karlen have provided a great resource for all of us who want to present our pro-life views in a reasoned, sensible manner. They show how to keep the main thing the main thing. You'll want to read this helpful little book again and again."

— Jim Daly, President, Focus on the Family

"It wasn't that long ago that abortion supporters stated their goal of 'safe, legal, and rare.' Now it's, 'Shout your abortion!' How can we address what the US Catholic bishops have called 'the preeminent moral issue of our time'? All who value the sanctity of life and try to promote a Culture of Life are indebted once again to 40 Days for Life for this new book. It gives us all practical advice on how to discuss this topic with friends, neighbors, family, and even those who disagree with us. A must-read!"

— Bishop Joseph L. Coffey, Archdiocese for the Military Services, USA

"As a pro-life OB/GYN, by the grace of God, I am blessed to minister to women outside abortion centers and treat patients with NaProTECHNOLOGY in my office. In the endless quest to educate myself, I have read many books about pro-life apologetics. This is the most insightful, easy-to-digest, and entertaining book that I have encountered on the topic. I believe that reading this book will empower pro-life individuals to speak kindly and respectfully with authority and love on every abortion-related topic. Lives will be saved because the end to abortion begins with one-on-one conversations that result in a change of hearts and minds. Read. Share. Go and pray outside!"

— Monique Ruberu, MD, OB/GYN

"*What to Say When* addresses an essential topic for our time. We face an erosion of the understanding of human life as a gift from God that literally threatens life at every stage. This reality makes it more essential than ever that we seek the tools we must use in order to change minds and hearts. I believe this text will prove to be essential reading for all who hold life sacred and are seeking ways to speak this truth clearly and boldly. Shawn is a man who has done much to foster the sanctity of life in our culture, and his voice speaking to these issues is a great blessing. Let us heed this message and go about the business of changing the world one heart at a time."

— Bishop Joseph Strickland, Diocese of Tyler

WHAT TO SAY
WHEN
THE COMPLETE NEW GUIDE
TO DISCUSSING ABORTION

Also by Shawn Carney

40 Days for Life: Discover What God Has Done,
Imagine What He Can Do (co-author)

The Beginning of the End of Abortion:
True Stories from the Global Movement
Happening in Your Neighborhood

To the Heart of the Matter: The 40 Day
Companion to Live a Culture of Life

Also by Steve Karlen

This Is When We Begin to Fight:
A Family's Battle Against Late-Term Abortion,
Academia . . . and Miscarriage at Home

WHAT TO SAY
WHEN

THE COMPLETE NEW GUIDE
TO DISCUSSING ABORTION

How to Change Minds and Convert Hearts
in a Brave New World

SHAWN D. CARNEY
AND
STEVE KARLEN

K|A
KOLBE & ANTHONY
PUBLISHING

Kolbe & Anthony Publishing
4112 East 29th Street
Bryan, TX 77802

ISBN: 978-1-7370477-1-1

Cover design: Jam Graphic Design
Interior layout and e-book: LParnell Book Services

Printed in the United States of America

28 27 26 25 24 23 22 21   1 2 3 4 5

To all those we labor alongside
in the trenches of this great cause.

ક્ષ ક્ષ ક્ષ

Contents

Love without truth is blind;
truth without love is empty.

— Joseph Ratzinger

❧ ❧ ❧

Foreword

As you have probably noticed, we live in a chaotic, distracted, media-saturated society, where many controversies vie for our attention. Sometimes it can be hard to know which way is up, much less which issues are truly important. Yet even amid all the noise, the most important and fundamental thing remains clear: life. Without life, we have nothing. Without the right to life, no other right can gain a foothold. If life is not worth defending, then nothing else can be worth defending. This is why abortion sits always at the center of the culture war. The peripheral arguments may change, each day may bring with it a new controversy du jour, but this fight endures. We cannot move on from it until it has been won.

But something else endures, too. Many pro-lifers, though they have positioned themselves on the right side of the issue, still are not equipped to argue the point persuasively. This is rather frustrating, and even tragic, because our point is not only absolutely crucial and true but also intuitively powerful. It has the benefit of both moral clarity and logical simplicity. It boils down to this: abortion intentionally and directly destroys innocent human life, and it is always wrong to intentionally and directly destroy innocent human life. There is plenty more to be said about the subject, and much more will be said in this book, but that is our case. The person who disagrees with this case has a much more daunting task in front of them. They must defend the proposition that intentionally and directly destroying innocent human life is sometimes good. Or else they must advance the even more absurd proposition that an unborn child somehow doesn't count as human, or a life, or innocent. Whichever way they go, the logical and moral challenge is insurmountable. Their position is, quite literally, indefensible. The job of the pro-lifer is to make the indefensibility of the contrary view vividly clear.

What to Say When is an indispensable tool for this rhetorical fight. It will not only give you a better and clearer grasp of your own arguments, but also prepare you to meet and rebut every conceivable pro-abortion talking point. Every time we engage with someone on the pro-abortion side, it is not merely a chance to win an argument, but an opportunity to shed a little light in the darkness and move one step closer to building a true culture of life. In that way, every debate about abortion is life or death. We cannot afford to lose and have no excuse to. Especially when we have this book, and the knowledge it contains, in our arsenal.

Matt Walsh
The Daily Wire

The Landscape Has Changed

If anything has ever made me want
to eat an aborted fetus, it's this law.
— Actress Sarah Silverman responding to a pro-life law

A group of PhD-level scientists on a panel at Texas A&M University awaited questions from students. They were all experts in their respective fields, and all volunteered to be on the panel for an open discussion.

The topic was abortion.

One male geneticist wandered outside of his field and claimed that women should have an abortion if they want. A student raised his hand and asked a question:

> *Student:* "Doctor, your work and research are so impressive and known to everyone in this room. Would you say that from your expertise, our DNA and genetic makeup are all there from the moment of conception?"
>
> *Geneticist:* "Yes, that is clear from science."
>
> *Student:* "So once conception occurs, we have a unique, unrepeatable human being."
>
> *Geneticist:* "Yes, correct."
>
> *Student:* "It just seems inconsistent for you as a scientist to prove life begins in the womb at

1

conception and yet believe we can take that life through abortion."

Geneticist: "Well, I can't let my professional scientific research influence someone's belief about human life."

The landscape on abortion has indeed changed. Gone are the days of abortion being viewed as a matter of religion (pro-life) versus freedom (pro-choice). It is now an issue of science (pro-life) versus emotion (pro-choice).

It is easy to study up or prepare for an academic abortion panel discussion like the one I (Shawn) witnessed as a student at Texas A&M. It is more difficult, and intimidating, to discuss abortion when it comes up in our daily lives. It always seems to be when we are busy with 101 other things we must do when, suddenly, the most crucial issue of our generation (and every generation after us) pops up out of the blue in conversation. We've been in the pro-life movement for a combined thirty-five years and have had thousands of conversations on abortion in various and occasionally comical settings. We know abortion comes up when you least expect it, and this book will help you calmly defend the most dehumanized humans in our world today in a simple and effective manner.

Much like the abortion issue, this book is easy and uncomplicated. You don't need any special insights or wisdom to be pro-life. Being pro-life is the most basic intellectual position on earth, and our ancestors (good and evil alike) couldn't imagine any other position. Nothing is more unnatural than abortion, and no common surgery is anywhere near as controversial, even fifty years after legalization. No other issue in the world is like abortion, and yet it occurs 73 million times worldwide every year.[1]

The ongoing controversy on the news, in politics, or at the Thanksgiving dinner table stems from the fact that we have not ultimately "gotten over" this fifteen-minute surgery. Abortion still troubles us when it comes up in everyday conversation, political debates, and sermons. This discomfort we have about abortion isn't because we have some innate desire to oppress women, but because we are inherently humane.

Life is easy to defend because abortion can only be justified by rejecting science, reason, and God (if you think He matters). That's why it is not bold for us to say that defending life is easy from an intellectual standpoint. In our desire to be respectful, we have given far too much intellectual credibility to abortion supporters' arguments.

But it is disrespectful to give credence to the defense of a barbaric procedure that kills an innocent person. We never give any credibility or respect to any other form of child abuse. Our pro-life convictions must come with confidence. Respecting someone doesn't mean giving his dilapidated view of human life credibility.

We must fight the temptation to think that love is possible without truth.

Just as important, we must fight the temptation to speak the truth without love, which only endangers the unborn children we are attempting to defend. Mother Teresa is not the only person in the world who can boldly speak up for the unborn to the most powerful in our world and still be viewed as a loving and caring person. You and I can do it too!

The Old Stereotypes Are Gone

As the abortion debate landscape has changed, many stereotypes have been annihilated by data from decades of legal abortion.

Abortion is not a battle between women and men. (After all, it was an all-male Supreme Court that legalized abortion.) Nor is it a fight between religion and freedom or the church versus the state. Gone is the stereotype of religious people as Pharisees who are blind to science as they force their morality on people. Now, it's pro-life Christians who appeal to science on behalf of unborn children.

The stereotype that abortion empowers women to be free has collapsed as well. Five decades of post-abortive women sharing their regret have proven that women are not victims of the pro-life movement; they are the leaders of it.

Any notion that abortion is legitimate medicine and a source of pride for the medical field has been exposed as a sick joke. Abortion providers are pariahs in their fields. Unlike oncology, cardiovascular care, orthopedics, pediatrics, or obstetrics, abortion is never something a hospital or medical school brags about being known for.

But it's not only abortion supporters' stereotypes that have been dismantled. Some pro-life stereotypes have been shot down too. Through the testimonies of former abortion work-ers, we know now that all abortion staffers are not on a mission to kill as many babies as possible. Some are, but many believe they are helping women. Tragically, their misguided intentions can take a lifetime to recover from. The exodus of abortion workers out of the abortion industry started with Dr. Bernard Nathanson and grows every year.

The point isn't just that abortion workers sometimes con-vert to being pro-life; it is that they convert *often*. Doctors, nurses, and other medical personnel do not stop believing in knee surgeries or wisdom-teeth removals and speak out against their industry. But many thousands of abortion workers have lost faith in their line of work, left their jobs, and are now rec-ognized for their courage.

New Stereotypes for Abortion Opponents

Socrates said, "Know thyself." It's good advice. As pro-lifers, we all need to know how we are perceived and how others perceive themselves.

Abortion supporters often paint pro-lifers as:

- Christian bigots
- hateful toward gays
- having no experience with abortion
- hateful toward poor people
- sexist
- racist
- living in the Stone Age
- brainwashed
- supportive of the death penalty
- in favor of "forced birth" (that's a thing now, and we will cover it)
- wanting to lock up women who have abortions
- wanting to lock up doctors who do abortions
- hypocrites
- uncaring toward children after birth
- intolerant
- judgmental
- Republican

New Stereotypes for Abortion Supporters

Abortion advocates often understand themselves as:

- open-minded
- LGBT-friendly
- enlightened
- tolerant
- pro-equality

- compassionate toward minorities
- educated
- Democrat

It doesn't matter whether you agree or disagree with these stereotypes. It doesn't matter whether you find them amusing or they offend you. We pro-lifers need to know these stereotypes exist so that we are not caught off guard when they are dropped on us. And we need to be prepared not to walk into a trap and get sidetracked into abandoning our conversation on abortion for a conversation on homosexuality, politics, the death penalty, or any number of other issues.

When we allow ourselves to be sidetracked, we play into abortion supporters' hands. Most abortion advocates love to go off topic because abortion is indefensible. Don't let them steer you off course, surprise you, or jar you when they label you. Labeling is expected, and we respond by staying the course and keeping the discussion focused on abortion.

The Heart Is the Key to the Mind

As we enter this book, know that this epic battle for life is ultimately won on our knees. Our prayers and fasting are our most powerful resources in this struggle.

Yes, it's true that you don't need to believe in God to be against abortion. Any reasonable person should be against abortion. Many atheists and agnostics are pro-life, and they should be. The intellectual case for abortion is easy to refute, and the beauty of life is easy to embrace.

But the abortion crisis goes much deeper. Many things have to go wrong for a woman to feel she has no other choice than to pay a doctor, a healer, to violently end the life of her baby. Even more must go wrong for that doctor to do it and for the state to approve of it—and to help pay for it.

This is a spiritual battle. When individuals and governments take it upon themselves to determine whether a person is worthy to live, we are forced to ask, and answer, the most basic and essential questions of human life: What is it? Where does it come from? And why is it sacred?

Ultimately, abortion survives not because its supporters make a strong case but because pain, confusion, and sometimes anger fuel a relentless push to keep it legal. That's why our hearts and the tone we use when discussing abortion are critical.

We don't know a single former abortion worker who was 100 percent pro-life when she walked out of her facility and asked for help leaving her job. But after leaving their jobs, these former workers' hearts were touched by the Christian charity they witnessed in pro-life prayer warriors. Love softens hearts and leads even the staunchest abortion supporters to the realization that life in the womb is real, inherently precious, and deserving of protection.

The landscape has indeed changed, and the stakes have never been higher. Let us guard our hearts, sharpen our minds, and always proceed with love as we defend the most innocent among us. Let's get started!

CHAPTER 1

Go on Offense

Love follows knowledge.
— St. Thomas Aquinas

Heated arguments never change hearts and minds. But calm, compassionate, true arguments do.

Contentious arguments easily stray off topic, making it difficult to articulate a commonsense case for life to those who have never heard one before or who adamantly reject any restriction on abortion.

While abortion is an emotional topic, take extra care to make sure your conversations on abortion don't become free-for-alls. Instead, stick to the basics: we live in a society that has legally and scientifically dehumanized an entire segment of our population—unborn children—in order to destroy and discard them for any reason, or for no reason at all.

Life doesn't need defending, but abortion does. Remember these three points to keep your abortion discussion on track *no matter what.*

Point 1: Keep Your Cool, but Don't Be a Wimp

We live in a world of two extremes when abortion comes up in conversation.

On one hand, we are tempted to remain silent out of fear of offending someone. In today's world, if you so much as hint that objective truth exists, you are dismissed as a bigoted, insensitive racist forcing your outdated beliefs on everyone around you. "Cancel culture" leads many to treat moral issues so delicately that we walk on eggshells, afraid to say anything substantive to anyone about any issue of significance.

Cancel culture has taken over media, corporate America, and pop culture to an extent nobody would have imagined only a few years ago.

So what?

Cancel culture is outside our control. We can't cower in fear and make half-hearted comments about abortion (like "it's a tough issue" or "everyone has their own view") out of fear we may be accused of being insensitive. To avoid speaking the truth about abortion is to cancel ourselves, and that's a greater tragedy than being canceled or censored by others.

Failing to stand up for unborn children isn't just cowardly; it has deadly consequences. We have heard countless stories of regret from people who passively opposed abortion—and then passively supported a friend or family member's decision to have an abortion. After the abortion is completed, there is no going back. Those people who had an opportunity to encourage an abortion-bound mom to choose life share the burden and the guilt of *not having said anything*.

On the other hand, some pro-lifers aggressively look for opportunities to boisterously (and sometimes obnoxiously) "declare the truth whether people like it or not because we will neither be silent nor stand by as the innocent are slaughtered."

We don't want to deliberately offend others in a misguided attempt to shock them into accepting the truth. We've certainly met some passionate pro-life people who come off as know-it-alls. They lose their credibility and their audience five seconds after they open their mouths. As we say in the South, "Bless their hearts."

Both approaches—passive nice guy and in-your-face truth teller—are disrespectful to those who support abortion and to those who are being aborted. Instead, a good measuring stick for evaluating your conversation with an abortion advocate is to ask yourself whether you made it clear you oppose abortion and whether you challenged the abortion supporter to reevaluate his or her position on the issue.

Reconciling truth with sensitivity is easier said than done and forever will remain a struggle for all of us. But that doesn't mean speaking the truth in love is impossible. It can be done and needs to be done. All the abortion workers we have talked to and have helped leave the abortion industry knew we were against abortion before, during, and after their conversions. They also knew we came from a place of love and sincerity.

Truth and love are not in two opposing camps. When bound together honestly, truth and love convert more hearts on more issues than any other approach. We can articulate the pro-life position without acting like self-righteous jerks. And we can do so with confidence.

Point 2: Don't Let Abortion Advocates Distract You

The only intellectually honest defense of abortion is the Machiavellian "might makes right" philosophy in which brute strength is the only measure of morality. This mindset is responsible for every holocaust, every genocide, and every human atrocity in history.

When discussing abortion, we must be disciplined and respectful. But respecting an abortion advocate does *not* require us to give credibility to his or her arguments.

Nor does respecting abortion advocates require us to address the many ridiculous hypothetical arguments used to justify killing an innocent baby. One famous argument compares an unborn baby to a kidnapper experiencing renal failure who takes you hostage to steal your kidney function.[1]

Another bizarre hypothetical situation concerns conjoined twins. After the twins are born, one becomes sick with a deadly virus. The other twin will become infected shortly thereafter, and both will die. Shouldn't we kill the twin with the deadly virus to save the other before he becomes infected? After all, the twin with the virus will die either way.

Abortion advocates in academia love to sit around and argue this garbage.

Don't take the bait. Getting into the weeds of hypothetical situations that rarely, if ever, take place is a waste of time and not the point of this book. This book is for reality. Instead, if someone in your life tries to justify abortion by appealing to hostage-taking kidney patients or conjoined twins, take control of the conversation by calling out his disingenuity.

What? Why do you need bizarre hypothetical scenarios to justify the most common surgical procedure in the world, which has been legal in the United States for fifty years and happens 73 million times worldwide every year? I can legally take my wife in to have a late-term abortion the day before my daughter's due date. Why do you feel the need to justify that with some ridiculous hypothetical?

In other words, don't get sucked into an argument that ignores reality. Can some dreamed-up hypothetical kidney disease argument spare a woman walking into Planned Parenthood right now decades of physical, emotional, and spiritual suffering?

Abortion advocates are often detached from the reality of abortion and the real scenarios that lead to abortion. We are not. Don't allow them to live in a fantasy world. Instead of addressing their self-serving hypotheticals, stay on topic and stick to the matter at hand: abortion kills an innocent child.

The Irish are known for being calm in hostile scenarios and hostile in calm scenarios. It is what led Sigmund Freud to say, "This is one race of people for whom psychoanalysis is of no use whatsoever." Try as you might, you can't rope an Irishman into an argument unless, of course, there is nothing to argue over. There is great value in refusing to engage abortion supporters on every absurd argument they throw at you. Dismissing the silliness allows you to keep first things first when giving a voice to those who have none but ours.

Point 3: Make Abortion Supporters Play Defense

"How do I defend life?"

"What do I say if . . . ?"

"How can I reach a person if he or she says . . . ?"

We've been asked these questions, and others like them, repeatedly. They're important questions and the reason for this book. But these questions assume that the burden of proof is on pro-lifers. Abortion supporters demand that *we* provide an explanation for our pro-life stance.

The opposite is true. Life needs no defense. Defending life is always the default position. You don't see cardiologists, oncologists, and trauma surgeons asked to justify their efforts to protect human life. Neither should pro-lifers be scrutinized for saving lives.

Instead, those who advocate killing and dismembering unborn children should be the ones on the hot seat, forced to justify their radical agenda.

Surgery and medication are meant to preserve or enhance life. Patients know that medical staff have invested years into training and education that will help *heal* them. If a doctor ends up killing a patient, he will be sued for malpractice—except for abortion.

Abortion turns health care on its head. Abortion is the only surgery on earth you are not supposed to survive. The abortion pill is the only pharmaceutical on the planet meant to kill a patient who didn't ask for it.

Think about it: if a baby survives an abortion, it means the doctor did something *wrong*.

Many politicians advocate, sometimes successfully, to deny health care to a baby girl who survived an abortion. That baby girl's crime was that she survived the arranged and negotiated taking of her life. Instead of celebrating that she survived the surgery designed to kill her, abortion doctors leave her on the table to die alone.

And still, abortion advocates take it for granted that you owe them an explanation for your pro-life views. It's time to turn the tables by going on offense and demanding an explanation for why it could ever be OK to kill a defenseless baby.

How do we go on offense? Ask questions that make abortion advocates answer for the grisly reality of abortion. Most people prefer talking to listening, so questions demonstrate respect for the person with whom you're debating abortion and create a space for a fruitful dialogue.

Many well-intentioned abortion advocates have never thought much about what abortion actually is. We, too, often think they have, but more often than not, they haven't. This applies even to some abortion workers. They have merely bought into vague euphemisms and slogans like "choice," "reproductive rights," and "privacy."

Many ill-intentioned abortion supporters, the coldest of the cold, don't care that it's a baby, see us as the enemy, and want abortion on demand—no restrictions and paid for by the government.

Both groups become vulnerable when you ask questions and then respectfully listen to their answers. Ask four or five questions to get the abortion supporter thinking before you reveal your own position. The more an abortion supporter talks early on in your conversation, the better. No matter what, do not interrupt or correct the person you're talking to.

Your questions shift the burden and put the pressure on the abortion supporter. You no longer have to be an encyclopedia of medical facts and abortion statistics. You might not need to say much at all as abortion advocates sometimes recognize the depravity and insanity of their answers to your questions.

Be confident because your position is the one that's true. Don't forget it.

What questions should you ask?

It depends how abortion came up in conversation. The following questions come in no specific order and have helped disarm abortion supporters ranging from strangers on the street to Planned Parenthood employees. Some are repetitive but worded in different ways; that is intentional:

- What is an abortion?
- Why do you support abortion?
- When are you comfortable with a baby being aborted? Is there a point in pregnancy when you would oppose abortion?
- Many people feel uncomfortable with a clearly pregnant woman at twenty-five weeks or thirty-five weeks of pregnancy having an abortion. What is your cutoff line for when a baby should not be aborted?

- Is your support for abortion (or any restrictions on abortion that you favor) based on science or more of a "gut" feeling?
- Do you think that the human dignity of babies in the womb increases over time?
- Are babies to you more valuable at twenty-five weeks than twelve weeks?
- Since abortion was legalized in 1973, do you ever feel like the science that supported legalizing it has become outdated?
- How do they actually do an abortion?
- As technology and science advance, medical journals report that babies can survive outside the womb at earlier and earlier points in pregnancy. But abortion laws have not adjusted accordingly. Are you OK with doing surgery on a twenty-two-week-old viable baby in the womb to improve his life but aborting a baby girl in the womb at the same age?
- Is the source of our human dignity the wishes our parents have for us?
- Do you believe that babies who are born into poverty are less valuable than babies born into wealth?
- Do you think that the actions of our parents—good or bad—make us any more or less valuable than people born with different parents?
- Do you feel that if a woman really wants an abortion but the baby survives and is born alive that the medical team, who attempted to abort the baby, should provide the newborn with medical care?
- Should baby girls and boys who survive abortion attempts get care if they cannot breathe on their own?

- Do you think infanticide is ever justified?
- Does everyone really deserve a chance at life, or can circumstances change that?
- Do you think babies in the womb with disabilities are stronger candidates for abortion?
- Should parents who find out their baby is disabled have priority access to abortion?
- Do you believe we get our human dignity at birth?
- Black Americans only make up around 13 percent of the population, but they make up 38 percent of all abortions. Do you think that is good or bad?
- Should corporate America use its power and wealth to help abort more babies in poverty-stricken countries in Africa?
- Do you think it is elitist or offensive to tell family-oriented cultures outside of the United States that they should not have children?
- Do you think there should be more medical alternatives for women who choose not to have an abortion?

As you listen patiently, sprinkle in, "Explain what you mean by that."

Notice these questions are not political or focused on abortion providers. They are aimed at the big-picture concept that drives abortion: might makes right. Most abortion advocates will not admit to supporting this mentality, but millions support it indirectly through their support for killing the most vulnerable members of the human family.

These questions will lead to the topics we equip you to handle in this book, including rape, the humanity of the unborn child, Planned Parenthood, politics, and many more.

What to Say to Go on Offense

1. Make the case for life courageously but politely, gently but firmly. Respect and love abortion supporters without giving credibility to their arguments.

2. Stay on topic and remain grounded in reality. Don't entertain absurd hypothetical situations.

3. Ask at least four questions, listen, respond, and ask at least four more questions to get the abortion supporter to actually think about his position.

CHAPTER 2

What *Not* to Say

*That's what Abel was saying when he got it
in the back from his own brother with a cane.*
— Archie Bunker, *All in the Family*, CBS

Meaningful conversations, whether they go well or not, leave us thinking later, "I wish I would have said this" or "I wish I would have thought of that." These post-discussion revelations and regrets only increase after emotionally charged conversations—especially when the topic is abortion. And the natural regrets are only trumped by "I wish I had *not* said that."

What we *don't* say can be even more important than what we *do* say. The points we *shouldn't* make often concede ground (without us even realizing it) or convey disrespect toward those we're debating. That's why it's essential to consider what *not* to say when abortion comes up.

Full disclaimer: we are guilty of having committed all these violations at one time or another. Many of these points sound good and roll off the tongue without a lot of thought. All of them, to some degree, are true. But they are either incomplete or insensitive—and therefore counterproductive to our goal of winning a heart and a mind for life.

None of these common statements are the worst thing you can say when discussing abortion, but they are among the most common well-intentioned but weak points pro-lifers make.

This chapter's five points not to make when discussing abortion, of course, exclude the obvious "deadly" sins of losing your temper, cursing, or directly insulting the person you are talking to. If you do any of these things, you need to chill out and apologize.

Point 1: "We Believe Life Begins at Conception"

No, we don't.

Our personal beliefs are irrelevant to abortion-minded women, abortion doctors, pro-choice voters, Planned Parenthood workers, and abortion supporters, who simply do not care about what we do or do not believe.

Fortunately, we don't need to *believe* life begins at conception the way our ancestors did. The early Christians had to *believe* life begins at conception. The flat earthers of the Middle Ages had to *believe* life begins at conception. Great minds and leaders throughout history—including Charlemagne, Constantine, Robert the Bruce, Pocahontas, and General George Washington—all had to *believe* that life begins at conception.

But we don't *believe* life begins at conception; we *know* it does.

That life begins at conception is a verifiable scientific fact that is taught in medical schools, written about in peer-reviewed medical journals, described in embryology textbooks, and, today, filmed with cameras and shown by *National Geographic*.

Belief has nothing to do with it. Life begins at conception. Period.

Yes, depending on what state or country we live in, we can take human life at thirty-five weeks, twelve weeks, or eight weeks. But in order to kill a baby, the baby must exist. And the baby can only exist if he or she has been conceived.

Our existence is the result of our conception. And conception always results in a baby—never in a dog, a stapler, or a cowboy boot.

When you state that life begins at conception as a matter of empirically proven fact rather than as a matter of religious belief, you turn the tables on abortion supporters. Confronted with the scientific reality of life beginning at conception, abortion advocates are inevitably and immediately forced to deny science if they wish to persist in their support for abortion.

Abortion supporters cannot claim the scientific high ground. Do not let them. In order to defend abortion, they must and will resort to bullying human beings who are small and defenseless. It's a might-makes-right philosophy that claims power over science and reason.

Point 2: "The Baby Could Become the Next . . . ."

Almost every pro-life person has imagined a baby destined for abortion could be the one who cures cancer, becomes the first woman president, or saves the rain forest.

Famous historical parallels are almost too tempting not to reference. You've probably heard many of the stories.

A pro-life advocate with an audience tells a relatable story about a normal couple with decidedly abnormal circumstances. The couple is poor, sick, running from Communists, or in danger of being abducted by aliens. You know the drill.

Whatever the circumstances, the husband and wife are barely getting by when the woman gets pregnant. The drama and suspense increase (as listeners sit on the edge of their seats) with the revelation that the couple receives a devastating prenatal diagnosis. Or the baby is destined to become a notorious criminal. Or Fascists bearing guns show up at the door. Or some other severe problem no human being could possibly bear.

Then comes the set-up question: "Given the circumstances, should this woman have an abortion?"

The intensity reaches a fever pitch when someone from the audience says, "Well, I can understand the difficult—"

Abruptly, the speaker cuts him off and blurts out, "Congratulations! You just aborted Beethoven!"

These stories are sensational, albeit interesting. Perhaps they turn on the proverbial light bulb for some people, but they are superficial. An abortion-vulnerable baby should not need to become the next Beethoven or cure cancer in order to avoid being dismembered and sucked into a vacuum.

What about the struggling moms who choose life without any "happily ever after"? Is the disabled child who can barely communicate less valuable than the child who beat the odds to write a book, compose great music, become president, or land on the moon? Is the mom who heroically resisted pressure to have an abortion any less of a hero because her son becomes a drug addict instead of a Navy SEAL?

Devaluing the special-needs child or the drug addict speaks more to our weakness than to theirs.

As pro-lifers, we value the right to life over perceived quality of life. We value people for their existence as fellow human beings—not because of what they contribute to society. Our arguments should reflect those values.

Abortion is equally tragic whether the child aborted is destined for greatness, for obscurity, or for suffering. We understand the interest in sensational stories, but the source of our value isn't our achievements but because each of us is a gift from God. She doesn't need to be the next Beethoven; she only needs to be who God made her to be. Whether your kid is at the top of his class or a dropout, he is loved, cherished, and unrepeatable.

We've met many parents who chose life at the last possible moment—even from the operating table or after ingesting the first abortion pill. Those moms and dads are often embarrassed they ever considered abortion and grateful to God that He rescued them from that dark place. They are grateful that their little one survived her abortion appointment. Not one of them questions whether choosing life was worth it depending on their child's future accomplishments.

We've aborted tens of millions of people who would have done many things—good and bad. But we will never know because our society disregarded their inherent human dignity before they took their first breath.

Point 3: "Rape Accounts for Only 1 Percent of All Abortions"

Ouch.

We hear this argument a lot. Even reading this book, you may be tempted to say, "But come on; rape literally accounts for 1 percent of all abortions,[1] and it is used to justify 73 million abortions around the world every year. People think most women having abortions are rape victims, and we need to correct that."

If so, you're not wrong. But when you dismiss abortion in cases of rape, you're conceding too much ground.

When an abortion advocate responds, "What if rape accounted for 100 percent of all abortions?" you're forced to go on defense. You've unnecessarily backed yourself into a corner and lost an opportunity to force the abortion supporter to defend killing defenseless children. Furthermore, you've unintentionally suggested a disregard for women who suffer the trauma of sexual assault. The abortion advocate will eat you alive.

It is true that rape accounts for only 1 percent of all abortions, and there is a way to expose abortion supporters for using the horror of rape to advance their agenda. In chapter 6, we will take you through the appropriate context for discussing rape and abortion step by step.

Point 4: "If a Woman Doesn't Want a Baby, She Should Practice Safe Sex"

You might as well say, "She should keep her legs closed!" and storm out of the room.

This argument is counterproductive on multiple fronts.

First, the "safe sex" argument is fundamentally flawed because it suggests contraception as a solution to abortion. In chapter 8, we'll show why contraception is no solution to the abortion crisis. The only way to truly practice safe sex is to pursue chastity and reserve sex for marriage.

Secondly, this argument lets men off the hook. "It takes two to tango," as the saying goes. Many abortions aren't the result of a woman who doesn't want a baby but of a father who doesn't want a baby and pressures or even forces his girlfriend or wife into aborting.

Third, this argument blames the woman for a past decision—and one she can no longer reverse. The safe sex ship has sailed, and there's no time machine that can allow her to go back and avoid becoming pregnant.

The abortion-minded woman is pregnant *now.* She needs help *now,* not advice about what she should have done seven weeks ago.

Whether you tell a woman she should have avoided pregnancy by practicing safe sex or chastity, you come across as judgmental—and just plain rude. Nobody would dream of saying, "If you don't want a knee replacement, you should have exercised more and eaten healthier when you were younger."

We all make mistakes. We all sin. What's done is done. Address a crisis pregnancy with a merciful and understanding heart.

Fourth, the safe sex argument is off topic. Avoid changing the subject from abortion to contraception access. Planned Parenthood supporters love to avoid discussing the barbarity of abortion. Don't let them off the hook! The abortion industry loves discussing contraception and is good at promoting it. Avoid taking the conversation in this direction at all costs.

Point 5: "Late-Term Abortion Is Worse Than Early Abortion"

Yes, late-term abortion is barbaric. So are all other abortions.

A major problem with focusing on late-term abortion is that most abortion supporters are against the procedure. (Even most of secular Europe prohibits late-term abortion.) When you center the discussion on second- and third-trimester abortions, you provide abortion advocates an opportunity to seize the "reasonable," "middle-ground," or "nuanced" position.

"I agree late-term abortion isn't ideal," the abortion supporter might respond, "which is why we need more government-funded access to abortion without zealots standing outside of clinics. When more women can get abortions earlier, we will be able to end late-term abortion."

There's nothing reasonable or nuanced about a position that allows for the intentional killing of *any* unborn baby.

When we start discussing gestational limits on abortion, we (unintentionally) suggest there is a point in pregnancy at which we are comfortable with a baby being violently torn apart. We allow abortion supporters to say, "I'm against late-term abortion; I'm not a monster. In fact, I saw my grandson's ultrasound at twenty-five weeks. He's so cute! He had ten fingers and ten toes! Who could do such a thing? But at ten weeks there is no real problem if that's what the woman decides."

There is a real problem for the grandson!

Early abortions might not be as *messy* as late-term abortions, but they are no less deadly.

We have helped and consoled thousands of women who have had abortions. Almost all of them knew how far along they were at the time of the abortion. None of them claimed that the age of their baby made their abortion any easier or harder to live with afterward.

If you've made any of these arguments, don't worry. Like we said, we, too, are guilty as charged. We have made points like these many times, and experience can be a harsh teacher.

But defending the unborn and knowing what to say is easier when you make a resolution of what *not* to say. It will help you control the direction of the conversation and have fewer regrets afterward.

What *Not* to Say when Abortion Comes Up

1. We "believe" life begins at conception.

2. The baby could become the next . . .

3. Rape accounts for only 1 percent of all abortions.

4. If a woman doesn't want a baby, she should practice safe sex.

5. Late-term abortion is worse than early abortion.

CHAPTER 3

Life Begins at Conception

*We really need to get over this love affair with the fetus
and start worrying about children.*
— Joycelyn Elders, former US Surgeon General

"It's not a life; it's a potential life."

"Pregnancy tissue."

"Fertilized egg."

"Clump of cells."

"A parasite."

"Product of conception."

There's only one way to justify abortion, and that's to dehumanize the baby being aborted.

Abortion supporters know this, which is why they've worked so hard to craft clever euphemisms designed to obscure the fact that terminating a pregnancy really means *terminating the life of a human being*. Planned Parenthood pays marketing professionals in tall buildings top dollar to engineer slogans, buzzwords, and catchphrases, all designed to make abortion sound like something other than what it is: a brutal act of violence against a tiny baby.

Of course, these poll-tested, focus-group-driven talking points don't reflect reality. (When is the last time you attended a pregnancy tissue shower?) But they have been remarkably effective at distracting tens of millions of Americans from a simple truth that any toddler knows: you should never *ever* hurt a baby.

The abortion industry's successful marketing of abortion is bad news.

The good news is that it isn't difficult to demonstrate the humanity of the unborn child. And when you do, the case for abortion collapses. Nearly every defense of abortion assumes that the fetus (or embryo or zygote) is not a human being endowed with human rights. After all, who would suggest that rape, disability, or poverty are good reasons to terminate a six-month-old baby?

Nobody! At least nobody—to borrow a phrase from philosopher Peter Kreeft—"outside of [insane] asylums and graduate schools."[1] And why is that?

Consider two teenage mothers. Alyssa is fifteen years old and has a year-and-a-half-old toddler. Madison is thirteen and eight weeks pregnant. For both girls, something has gone terribly wrong. A criminal act has been committed as both teens became pregnant years before the age of consent. And now, both will face the same obstacles to completing their educations, going to college, and pursuing careers.

The same abortion supporters who would insist that Madison's best option to preserve her future is a safe, legal abortion would recoil in horror at the suggestion that Alyssa drown her baby in the bathtub to help ensure she remains on track to earn a university scholarship.

Again, the question is "why?"

The difference is that while pro-choicers recognize the obvious truth that Alyssa's toddler is a human being with a right to life, they somehow see Madison's unborn baby as unhuman—or at least *less* human.

That's why demonstrating the humanity of the fetus is so critical. When you prove that the fetus is indeed what Pope

St. John Paul II called a "single, unique, and unrepeatable"[2] human being, you win hearts and change minds. Here are three points that will help you do just that.

Point 1: Science Is Clear about When Life Begins

Pro-abortion progressives love to tout their devotion to science (often while insisting that a boy who wants to be a girl *actually* is a girl, but that's another book).

Fortunately, the pro-life position that life begins at conception is settled science. "[T]he fact that after fertilization has taken place a new human has come into being is no longer a matter of taste or opinion," wrote Dr. Jerome Lejeune. ". . . it is plain experimental evidence."[3]

Those aren't words in an evangelical preacher's Sunday sermon or of the pope quoting Catholic dogma, but from a world-renowned scientist and physician widely regarded as "the father of modern genetics."

When pro-lifers say, "We believe life begins at conception," abortion supporters dismiss the argument as a religious belief that can be disregarded in a secular society defined by a supposed separation of church and state. But a key distinction must be made: pro-lifers don't defend unborn children because our faith teaches us life begins at conception. Rather, because science affirms that unborn babies' lives begin at conception, our faith compels us to defend them.

Some abortion supporters dodge the matter by suggesting the issue of when life begins remains unanswered and therefore irrelevant. That's how the United States Supreme Court majority justified its sweeping fifty-state abortion legalization in *Roe v. Wade*. Writing for the court, Justice Harry Blackmun wrote, "We need not resolve the difficult question of when life begins. When those trained in . . . medicine, philosophy, and theology are unable to arrive at any consensus, the judiciary, at this point in the development of man's knowledge, is not in a position to speculate as to the answer."[4]

It was a ridiculous argument fifty years ago, and it's only gotten worse as science has gotten better.

But even if you set aside the mountain of scientific evidence proving the fetus is a human being, the burden of proof rests with the abortion industry. When in doubt, the only reasonable approach is to err on the side of *not* taking human life.

Imagine, for a moment, a deer hunter who has spent his entire day in the woods, waiting to bag a trophy buck. As dusk approaches, it seems he'll go home empty handed. He's growing restless. Just then, he sees movement in the bushes, fires his gun, and . . .

. . . kills his hunting buddy.

Would any judge accept as a defense Justice Blackmun's reasoning that our hunter friend "need not resolve the difficult question" of whether it was human life—or something else—on the other end of the gun barrel? Of course not. And today, we have incontrovertible proof that the fetus is human life. Dr. Lejeune is hardly the only revered scientist to confirm life begins at conception. The late Dr. Hymie Gordon, former Genetics Department chair at Mayo Clinic;[5] the National Bioethics Advisory Commission;[6] a distinguished professor at Harvard;[7] and many other leading universities agree. In fact, a 2018 academic study by University of Chicago researcher Dr. Steven Jacobs found that 95 percent of biologists (including supermajorities of scientists who self-identify as "prochoice" or "liberal") affirm that life begins at fertilization.[8] It's Embryology 101.

But you don't need a PhD to prove an unborn child is a living human being. All you need to do is prove two things:

The fetus is alive.

The fetus is human.

Let's quickly tackle them one at a time.

The Fetus Is Alive

It would be absurd to suggest a fetus is anything other than alive because the fetus (or the embryo or even a single-celled zygote) is growing. Cell division is taking place. The unborn child is processing nutrition. None of these biological processes take place in a nonliving entity. A rock neither moves independently nor metabolizes calories. A living being does.

And by the time a woman shows up at an abortion facility, the signs of life are even more obvious. Her child's heart starts beating by just twenty-two days, and brain waves are detectable shortly thereafter.

While the term *fetus* is simply Latin for "offspring," the term sounds sterile—more fitting for a robot than a living organism. There's a reason abortion-bound moms change their minds after learning their babies have ten fingers and ten toes: this simple fact illustrates that the fetus isn't some inanimate object but nascent life.

The Fetus Is Human

This, too, is easy to prove. A living creature cannot transform into a different species. It's the height of absurdity to insist a simple change in location from the womb into the world turns a nonhuman creature into a human being. An unborn child has a human genome—twenty-three pairs of distinctly human chromosomes composed of uniquely human DNA.

I (Steve) once participated in a public debate with an abortion advocate who accepted my premise that the fetus is both alive and human, even from the earliest stages of pregnancy.

However, she then made a curious comment. "Every time you wash your hands, living skin cells go down the drain," she said. "And nobody thinks it's murder to wash your hands. We're only talking about a few cells—just like with abortion."

My time with the microphone was finished, so I didn't have the chance to note that my opponent's argument was completely incompatible with observable human experience. Nobody mourns nor regrets washing her hands. But countless women spend decades grieving their abortions—not to mention marching, speaking, forming support groups, volunteering, and praying in honor of the lives their abortions ended.

So, what's the fundamental difference?

The difference is that when a mother washes her hands, she remains very much alive—even if she loses a few of her own skin cells in the process. But if she has an abortion, a life is lost. The heart that stops beating is not her own heart but the heart of a unique, individual member of the human race.

The clear and compelling proof that a new human being comes into existence at conception means that the pro-abortion caricature of pro-life Christians as uneducated, superstitious bumpkins who reject modern science has it *exactly backward*. The real superstition is to suggest that a fetus magically becomes a living human being simply by passing through the birth canal.

Hardly. If there is any question as to whether the being you propose to kill is human, the only acceptable approach is to err on the side of life. Those who claim a human fetus is anything other than a living human being (or even those who suggest the matter is open for debate) are science *deniers*. We need to be willing to charitably call them out on it. Pro-lifers should shout from the rooftops that science is on *our* side.

Point 2: Support for Abortion Is Discrimination against Tiny Human Beings

Once you prove beyond a reasonable doubt that the unborn child is a human being, many abortion supporters will try to move the goalposts. "Sure, the fetus might be a human being, but it's not a person."

According to this line of thinking, a fetus—though human—should not be legally considered a person, typically because he or she lacks consciousness, self-awareness, and the capacity for transcendent thought. (Bizarrely, some of the same ethicists in favor of denying personhood to unborn babies would grant legal personhood to advanced mammals or even robots!) Without the benefit of the status of legal personhood, an unborn child has no legal rights, including the right to life.

But is it true that one must demonstrate consciousness, self-awareness, and the capacity for transcendent thought to be a person? Isn't simply being human enough?

We turn, again, to Peter Kreeft, who notes there is a clear difference between what a person *does* and what a person *is*: "One cannot function as a person without being a person, but one can surely be a person without functioning as a person. In deep sleep, in coma, and in early infancy, nearly everyone will admit there are persons, but there are no specifically human functions such as reasoning, choice, or language."[9] Kreeft's reasoning applies to other stages of life as well. Old age, Alzheimer's disease, and disability might rob a person of certain uniquely human capabilities, but those who suffer from such conditions don't cease to be persons. And even among people who are in possession of all their human faculties, the differences in ability that exist naturally from person to person mean that some people are able to exercise those faculties at higher levels than others. But nobody suggests that a member of society who is more intellectually gifted than another is somehow more of a person.[10]

When abortion supporters argue that not all human beings are persons under the law, they are treading on *very* dangerous ground. Our society is well versed in bitterly divisive debates over which human beings are entitled to human rights.

Progressives often boast that they are on the "right side of history." But if there's one lesson we learn from slavery and the Jim Crow era, the Trail of Tears, ethnic cleansing, racial segregation, internment camps, and genocide, it's that history never looks back fondly on those who fought to deny basic human rights to a particular class of human beings. Instead, it's those who fought in defense of the dehumanized, the disenfranchised, and the persecuted who are vindicated in the history books.

Progressives' demand for equality, inclusiveness, and justice rings hollow when it's accompanied by the battle cry of "free abortion on demand!" Abortion supporters are quick to heap scorn upon their ancestors for brutalizing African slaves because they looked different, but they have no problem brutalizing unborn children for the exact same reason.

"It's only an inch-and-a-half-long clump of cells," the abortion advocate observes. "Are you seriously telling me that's a person?" If a pre-born child is a clump of cells, so are you and I. The main difference is that we're bigger! Long after birth, babies, toddlers, children, and teenagers all continue to grow and develop, but they do not become more human. Their lives do not become more valuable as they get bigger.

The same abortion advocate who compared abortion to handwashing admitted her prejudice against unborn children when she heard my case for the personhood of the fetus, shrugged, and said, "I just don't *feel* like it has the same value as someone who's been born."

She probably didn't realize what a stunning admission she had made by acknowledging that her disregard for the lives of unborn children wasn't based in reason or science or philosophy or even in law, but in her own personal, subjective *feeling.* She didn't stop to think that if she can deny a human being's personhood based on a feeling, what is to stop anybody else from denying the personhood of an entire category of people?

When discussing abortion with progressives, we need to hold them accountable to their own standards. If their call for equality doesn't include every member of the human family— born and unborn—it's dishonest. Discrimination against the small, weak, and vulnerable is the most contemptible and dangerous form of discrimination there is.

Point 3: Abortion Supporters' Anti-Science Claims Don't Hold Up to Scrutiny

Some zealous abortion defenders can be relentless in questioning pro-lifers and our motives. Like a detective in a police interrogation room, pro-choice advocates scrutinize your every response looking for that "gotcha!" moment they can use to justify all abortions. It doesn't matter how many questions you articulately and compassionately answer; there's always one more point your interrogator thinks will prove him right once and for all. "Well, what about an impoverished, disabled eleven-year-old, non-English-speaking immigrant who gets pregnant by a family member while also battling a particularly aggressive form of cancer such that she'll die without an abortion?"

We don't provide such an extreme example to make light of tragically desperate situations. Pro-lifers on sidewalks and in pregnancy centers around the world make incredible sacrifices to provide support and solutions for mothers in extraordinarily difficult situations. It's the abortion industry that uses real moms facing real crises as political pawns to sell abortions.

Nevertheless, it's important to provide answers—especially when the questions are sincere. But when it comes to addressing the humanity of the unborn child, we need to turn the tables and ask the abortion supporter some hard questions.

Abortion advocates are rarely logical in their defenses of abortion. When they find themselves unable to craft a cohesive response to your simple questions, the honest ones will reassess their stance.

"OK, so you disagree with me and with 95 percent of credentialed biologists when they say that human life begins at conception. What do *you* think a fetus is?"

"It's not a life; it's a potential life."

"You didn't really answer my question. Saying it's a potential life means it could become a life. But a potential life must be an actual something. What do you think it is right *now?*"

"It's just a blob of cells."

"Are those cells living?"

"I guess."

"Are they living, human cells?"

"Sure."

"So, the fetus is a human life?"

Now, you probably aren't going to see your debate partner immediately recognize the error of his ways and acknowledge an unborn child's humanity. But you've given him something to think about, planting the first seeds of eventual conversion. And if your discussion is in public, you made a powerful impression on any spectators who might not have given much thought to the issue of abortion.

Asking questions can be particularly helpful when you encounter "moderate" abortion supporters who take a "middle-of-the-road" pro-choice stance designed to find common ground. For example, many pro-choice people will attempt to stake out a moderate approach by saying, "I think abortion is a woman's choice, but I do agree with you that it should be rare. It's definitely not something to be taken lightly." When abortion supporters make this argument, they're trying to sound nuanced, reasonable, and sophisticated. In reality, they're taking the most unreasonable position imaginable.

Why?

Many abortion supporters don't actually believe it's OK to kill a human being; they're just dead wrong on their science when they claim a fetus isn't a human being. And abortion enthusiasts who acknowledge the humanity of the fetus but claim a might-makes-right authority to kill an unborn child are at least honest in admitting they believe murder isn't intrinsically wrong. But moderate pro-choicers are making a logically indefensible argument: killing innocent babies is wrong, but we should allow it anyway.

Respond by calling the question: *Why* should abortion be rare?

Nobody suggests that knee replacements, appendectomies, or *any* other surgery should be rare. Either the fetus is not a human person and has no moral significance, or she is an innocent human person, and nothing could ever justify intentionally ending her life. There's no more schizophrenic position than to suggest abortion should be legal but rare. It's no more sensible than saying, "Yes, Africans are human beings, and I think we should only subject them to slavery *once in a while*."

The same principle applies when abortion advocates suggest a reasonable-sounding compromise by proposing a gestational time limit on abortion. "I could concede that late-term abortion is wrong," many admit. "But the cutoff should be twenty weeks." Again, you can simply ask, "Why?"

"So, you're OK with legal abortion at nineteen weeks and six days??"

"That's right."

"But not at twenty weeks?"

"You have to draw the line somewhere."

"So, what changes at twenty weeks?"

"I just feel like it's more of a baby at that point."

"Let me get this straight: at nineteen weeks, six days, it's not a baby, but the moment the clock strikes midnight, the fetus suddenly becomes a baby. How does that work?"

You might or might not persuade your pro-choice friend, but at the very least, you've demonstrated that the pro-life position is reasonable. It's abortion defenders who have to grasp at gut feelings, pseudoscience, and arbitrary gestational milestones to make their case.

꙼

Demonstrating that the fetus is a human being with human rights is an essential first step toward cutting through the abortion industry's spin.

When you prove the humanity of the unborn child, you also change public perception of pro-lifers. Opposition to abortion becomes not only a reasonable position but a compelling one. That shift saves moms and babies from abortion.

What to Say When Abortion Supporters Claim We Don't Know When Human Life Begins

1. Science is on our side. Life begins at conception.

2. Justice is on our side. Abortion is discrimination.

3. Abortion supporters have no cogent response to the scientific reality that life begins at fertilization.

CHAPTER 4

"My Body, My Choice"

*If I see a case . . . after twenty weeks, where it frankly is a child
to me, I really agonize over it because the potential is so imminently
there. . . . On the other hand, I have another position, which
I think is superior in the hierarchy of questions, and that is,
"Who owns this child?" It's got to be the mother.*

— Dr. James MacMahon, abortion provider

"My body, my choice" is, perhaps, the most popular message on handmade signs at any pro-choice rally.

The message is a pithy articulation of the "bodily autonomy" argument, which suggests that women have a right to *complete* control over their own bodies. This right is considered so fundamental that even the life of a vulnerable child—*her* vulnerable child—comes second to a woman's total sovereignty over her body. In this line of thinking, abortion is sacrosanct because it secures a woman's bodily autonomy by allowing her to end a pregnancy at any time and for any reason.

The catchier and snider version of "My body, my choice"— and one of our favorite pro-abortion slogans—is the classic "Keep your rosaries off my ovaries." Not only does it rhyme, but it insults religion too—the total package. We enjoy this message because it acknowledges (intentionally or not) that prayer is a threat to the future of abortion.

The bodily autonomy argument in favor of abortion takes many forms. Let's review and refute some of the most common.

Point 1: Abortion Advocates Actually Think Men Should Have a Voice on the Matter

Abortion supporters have an interesting and inconsistent relationship with men—and they don't usually realize it. On one hand, they say men need to get lost—that men simply shouldn't have a voice on a "women's issue." The corollary to "My body, my choice" for men is "No uterus, no opinion."

In some ways, it makes sense. After all, men can't have abortions, nor do they have to deal with all the large and small sufferings that accompany pregnancy:

- morning sickness
- countless visits to the doctor
- labor pains
- weight gain
- stretch marks
- late-night feedings

Once pregnancy occurs, men can (and many shamefully do) abandon their girlfriends to raise their children as single mothers. Why should men have a say on abortion when they can just leave?

But while abortion supporters are quick to dismiss and disregard the views of pro-life men, they happily welcome input from male abortion supporters. Planned Parenthood has never rejected a donation from a man because abortion is a women's issue. Advocates seem to forget that abortion was legalized and continues to be sustained by *men*:

- An all-male Supreme Court legalized abortion in 1973.
- Most abortion doctors are men.
- Men own most abortion facilities.
- Most politicians passing and enforcing pro-abortion laws are men.

It's disingenuous to suggest that abortion is exclusively a women's issue. From conception forward, pregnancy, abortion, and childbirth directly involve and impact men:

- Without a man, a baby does not come into existence.
- Nearly half of all children aborted are little men. (The rise of sex-selection abortions targeting girl babies means that countries like China now have 30 million-plus more men than women.[1] This isn't exactly a victory for women's rights or feminism.)
- Nobody benefits from abortion more than selfish men. Abortion subjects women to the trauma of a barbaric and invasive surgery. And once the abortion is completed, the promise of relief is nowhere to be found. But promiscuous men love abortion—and they should—because they gain the most. Abortion enables a bad man to use women for his own selfish pleasure and to wash his hands of guilt, convinced that abortion was the woman's decision.

Nobody has a right to silence someone's voice based on sex or gender. If you are a man and are told you have no voice in the abortion debate because you possess a *Y* chromosome, call it out as discrimination. Men and women have equal rights to take a position on every important social and political issue.

Of course, these days you also have the option of *identifying* as a woman for the duration of the abortion discussion.

Joking aside, if an abortion supporter who claims abortion is exclusively a women's issue also subscribes to gender ideology, don't be afraid to point out the irony. We once saw a pro-abortion sign that said, "Women's rights over fetuses every time.*" The fine print near the asterisk read, "And men with uteruses."

Is abortion a men's issue when it comes to "men with uteruses"? Do "women without uteruses" have a say on abortion? And if gender is nonbinary, a matter of choice, or otherwise untethered to biological sex, what in the world does being male or female have to do with abortion anyway?

Abortion supporters often claim that a woman's ability to conceive and bear a child renders her unable to compete with men in school and the workforce. Under this inverted worldview, a woman's reproductive abilities are actually looked upon as a disability—a disability that only abortion and contraception can remedy.

But the notion that a woman (who can bear children) must become more like a man (who cannot) to achieve equality suggests that women are inherently defective. This is misogynism at its worst. It's also an insult to the countless women who have achieved professional, academic, and artistic success while rearing children. Instead of telling a woman she'll be inferior to men unless she kills her child, we should encourage, support, and celebrate her for her unique ability to create human life *and* to pursue her other ambitions.

Point 2: Bodily Autonomy Does Not Mean Autonomy over Another Person's Body

"My body, my choice" sounds perfect if we ignore scientific and biological facts.

To have an abortion, you must be pregnant. That's the first requirement. You can't have an abortion without a baby—

a living, human child who has a unique set of DNA and who is a distinct biological organism from the mother having the abortion. There's a saying that, "My right to swing my fist ends where your nose begins." That adage applies to abortion: your right to do what you choose with or to your body ends where the body of your child begins.

As deeply as abortion impacts a woman, her body is impacted secondarily. Her body is the *setting* for the abortion. In other words, the abortion will be done on the baby, not the woman. It's the baby who experiences the primary effects of abortion, and it's the baby's body that is affected directly.

The heart stopped by abortion belongs to the baby, not to the mother. Abortion tears the baby's limbs apart, not the mother's limbs. The aftermath of an abortion is the lifeless body of the baby, not of the mother.

The baby has no power. He or she is at the mercy of the parents. It is not the woman's body that gives her the choice to have an abortion; it is the woman's will—or the will of the person forcing her to abort. That means the baby's very survival depends entirely on his mother's will.

The sign should accurately read, "My *will*, my choice."

But the baby depends on the woman's body for survival; therefore, abortion is a matter of her body and her choice, right? The baby does depend on the mother for survival. But our rights and our dignity don't change according to how dependent we are on others. All children remain dependent on their parents for nearly two decades after birth. Many disabled adults are dependent on their parents or other caretakers, but they retain their right to life.

If being dependent on your mom means that your life can be taken from you, then we have some old college buddies who live in their moms' basements who need to watch their backs.

In a *60 Minutes* interview, late-term abortion doctor Leroy Carhart stated, "My belief is that the unborn child is a parasite."[2] (Note that Carhart uses the term "unborn child." It wasn't a slipup. He has called the baby a "baby" many times.)

Is Carhart wrong? Does the baby have no rights because he is a parasite to the woman's body? When is the last time you attended a "parasite shower" for an expectant mother?

Carhart may be a doctor—and one who backs up his loud, proud advocacy for abortion by being one of the few physicians willing to do late-term abortions. But he doesn't know (or perhaps doesn't care) what he's talking about. It doesn't require a medical-school education—a grade-school textbook is enough—to know that a parasite is an organism of a *different* species from its host.

The baby is not a different *species* from the mom. The baby is not a giraffe or dolphin. The baby (who, again, Carhart has no problem calling a "baby") is not a fungus or an insect sucking life from the mother.

Abortion supporters use the word *parasite* to drive a wedge between mothers and their children. There's no relationship closer or more intimate than the relationship between a mother and her child. That's what makes abortion so unnatural, and it's a problem for those who try to justify abortion.

In order to market abortion to the masses, supporters need to create a break, a divorce, between mothers and their unborn children. Labeling an unborn baby a "parasite" is the perfect way to do this. It suggests that a child in utero is not a mother's flesh-and-blood offspring but an enemy, an intruder, or an attacker. The unborn baby is seen not as a child to be loved but as a foe to be feared.

When abortion supporters dehumanize the unborn child, they make it easier to kill that child. This dehumanizing language closely mirrors the racial and ethnic slurs used to dehumanize and destroy unwanted categories of people in genocides and human rights atrocities throughout history.

Dehumanization is always a great moral evil—and the shame of any society that practices it. It's even more unthinkable when mothers are conditioned to dehumanize not some random stranger but their own child.

Point 3: Bodily Autonomy Is Never Absolute

In recent years, abortion supporters have tried to rebrand the pro-life position as pro-"forced birth." We didn't make this up; if you haven't heard this one yet, you will.

The goal is to paint pro-lifers as bullies who oppress women by "forcing" them to give birth. The forced-birth meme suggests that *any* limit to abortion is an offense against bodily autonomy akin to slavery. It's a clever talking point. But it prompts some other questions about laws on the books that nobody challenges:

- Is a law that bans infanticide "forced parenthood"?
- Is a law that prevents child starvation "force-feeding"?
- Is a homicide law that prohibits you from killing the guy next door when his dog barks at night an unjust "forced neighbor" statute?

Aside from abortion, there are countless examples of largely uncontroversial laws that restrict what we can do with our bodies:

- We have to wear a seat belt on our bodies.
- We can't streak through the neighborhood with naked bodies.
- We can't shoot heroin into our bodies.

- We can't consume alcohol in certain locations.
- We can't stand up as our plane is taking off.
- We can't work out in the Dallas Cowboy training facility (even if we dress like and "self-identify" as Dallas Cowboys).
- We can't place our bodies in a busy intersection in support of Planned Parenthood.

If you were arrested for any of these acts and used "My body, my choice" as a legal defense, you'd be laughed out of the courtroom. What makes abortion different?

Don't take "My body, my choice" or any other bodily autonomy argument seriously and let it gain traction.

What to Say When "My Body, My Choice" Comes Up in Various Forms

1. Abortion isn't about a woman's body but the baby's. The woman can't abort her own body.

2. The baby has his or her own unique body, DNA, unrepeatable genetic makeup, heartbeat, and organs.

3. Bad and irresponsible men benefit the most from abortion. They are the winners.

4. Our dependency upon someone else does not diminish our equality or human dignity.

5. Every day we follow laws that restrict what we can do with our bodies.

CHAPTER 5

Can Abortions Be Medically Necessary?

I will not give to a woman
a pessary to cause an abortion.
— Hippocrates, the *Hippocratic Oath*

Is abortion health care?

In 2019, actress Miley Cyrus made headlines by posting a bizarre Instagram photo of herself licking a cake decorated with the words "Abortion is healthcare."[1] Controversy erupted—but not for the reason you might expect.

Self-described feminist baker Becca Rea-Holloway objected to Cyrus's photo, requesting financial restitution on the grounds that the actress ripped off her idea for an "Abortion is healthcare" cake. Before long, high-power attorneys writing for esteemed publications chimed in to assess whether Cyrus had infringed on Rea-Holloway's rights.[2]

But the flurry of abortion cake media coverage missed the infinitely more important question: are Cyrus and Rea-Holloway correct when they claim that killing an unborn child is a medical procedure of the same nature as, say, performing a biopsy or setting a broken bone?

Of course not. But don't take our word for it. Just ask Alan Guttmacher, MD, "the father of Planned Parenthood." As far back as 1967, Dr. Guttmacher wrote, "Today it is possible for almost any patient be brought through pregnancy alive,

unless she suffers from a fatal illness such as cancer or leuke-
mia, and, if so, abortion would be unlikely to prolong, much
less save, life."[3]

Nevertheless, in recent years, the assertion that abortion
is health care has become one of the abortion lobby's favored
talking points for three reasons:

1. *It removes the stigma of abortion. Roe v. Wade* handed
   abortion supporters a sweeping victory that legalized
   abortion on demand across the country. But it's a victory that has always been tenuous. Nearly five decades
   after *Roe*, abortion remains the most controversial topic
   in American public discourse.

   The same week Cyrus posed for her abortion cake
   photoshoot, Gallup polled Americans on the subject,
   revealing that the pro-life movement has made major
   public opinion gains—a troubling development for the
   abortion industry. Roughly half of all Americans sur-
   veyed on the legality of abortion now self-identify as
   "pro-life," compared with only 33 percent in 1995.[4]

   Like most public polling on abortion, Gallup's
   survey results revealed the American public's schizophrenic views on abortion. While 60 percent of Americans want to see *Roe v. Wade* upheld, just 44 percent
   say abortion is a morally acceptable decision.[5] In other
   words, while Americans reluctantly support the *right to
   have an abortion*, they don't like abortion itself.

   But everybody likes health care, which is why
   Planned Parenthood advocates believe that if they can
   just repeat the mantra "Abortion is health care!" enough
   times, Americans will finally embrace abortion without
   reservation.

2. *It makes abortion mainstream.* When people consider what abortion really is and what it looks like, they are horrified. That's why most pregnancy terminations aren't done in hospitals and doctors' offices. Even pro-choicers don't like the idea of going in for a routine physical and knowing that a baby is being dismembered across the hall. Abortion providers are pariahs in the medical community, and few health-care professionals want to share a practice with a physician who specializes in abortion.

Instead, most abortions take place in facilities operated by chains like Planned Parenthood or in stand-alone abortion businesses, which don't provide a full array of primary or specialty care. Abortion exists on the fringe of society, and its supporters hope that by equating abortion with health care they can bring it from the margins to mainstream hospitals and clinics.

3. *It bulldozes opposition.* The abortion lobby isn't content to merely make abortion mainstream. It also wants to crush dissent. The assertion that abortion is health care is often used to push for legislation requiring
   - religious hospitals to provide abortions,
   - health insurance plans to pay for abortions, and
   - pro-life medical personnel to perform abortions— regardless of conscientious objection.[6] (The ACLU has actually sued Catholic hospitals for refusing to perform abortions.[7])

The claim that abortion is health care has become doctrine for the pro-abortion movement. But it's a claim you can debunk when you remember these three points.

Point 1: Health Care Is Healing, Not Killing

The purpose of health care is simple: to restore and maintain the proper functioning of the human body. If something doesn't restore or maintain that proper functioning, it isn't health care.

A woman's body is designed for pregnancy. When she conceives and bears life, her reproductive system is working as it's meant to work. But abortion's sole purpose is to thwart or break the reproductive system—the exact opposite of health care. If abortion is health care, bulimia is nutrition.

Abortion advocates often respond by arguing abortion is necessary in cases where an expectant mother's health is threatened by her pregnancy. The abortion-promoting Guttmacher Institute cites depression, advanced maternal age, toxemia, and—most commonly—"feeling too ill during the pregnancy to work or take care of their children" as the chief health conditions that drive women to have abortions.[8]

But a mother's concern for her own health only drives 4 percent of abortions. It is disingenuous to use the health-of-the-mother argument to justify all abortions when up to 96 percent of abortions have nothing to do with the mother's health.[9]

Of course, that's not to say we can just write off those moms who do struggle with illness during pregnancy. Their health conditions can be severe and need to be taken seriously. But abortion is an inhumane and inappropriate response. Pregnancy termination as a cure for preeclampsia makes no more sense than decapitation as a treatment for a headache.

Instead, a woman who is ill during pregnancy deserves a solution that doesn't involve killing her baby. There's nothing compassionate about telling her the best we can do—the best we're willing to do—is to take her money and kill her baby. Fortunately, life-affirming treatments for the full array of physical and mental health difficulties are available, and pregnancy help centers can often direct moms in need to doctors willing to provide those life-affirming treatments at no charge.

If you've ever been near a pro-abortion demonstration, you've probably heard the chant, "Pro-life is a lie; you don't care if women die." It's a catchy jingle, but the claim that abortion saves lives just isn't true. Even in rare cases when pregnancy involves life-threatening complications, the direct killing of a pre-born child is never necessary to save the life of the mother.

Sometimes legitimate medical treatment *inadvertently* harms the pre-born child in order to save the life of a mother. For example, chemotherapy for a mother with cancer might *unintentionally* end a pre-born child's life, but this is an entirely different scenario from showing up to Planned Parenthood and paying six hundred dollars for an abortion (which, by the way, would do nothing to treat the mother's cancer) because the unborn child's death is an unwanted side effect.

According to former abortion provider Dr. Anthony Levatino, "In most such cases, any attempt to perform an abortion 'to save the mother's life' would entail undue and dangerous delay in providing appropriate, truly life-saving care." Levatino said that he terminated many pregnancies under the cover of saving mothers' lives, but that "In all those cases, the number of unborn children that I had to deliberately kill was zero."[10]

When abortion is seen as a legitimate response to a health challenge, not only does it end a human life; it lessens medical professionals' incentive to try to treat health conditions during a pregnancy. Abortion becomes an easy default recommendation for doctors afraid of difficulties or lawsuits.

But the goal of medicine should be to try to save both patients. In 1998, three separate doctors told Suzanne Guy she needed an abortion to save her own life. Suzanne refused and found doctors who were willing to fight for both Suzanne and her daughter Rachel. The two now co-lead the 40 Days for Life vigil in Marietta, Georgia.

Point 2: Legal Abortion Is Dangerous

Abortion supporters often argue that women will get abortions whether it's legal or not. Therefore, they say, we need to keep abortion legal to ensure it remains regulated and safe. Some even go so far as to claim that keeping abortion legal is pro-life because it will save the lives of women who would otherwise die from illegal, back-alley, coat-hanger-induced abortions.

One problem with this claim is it's false. The late former abortionist Dr. Bernard Nathanson, a pivotal player in the legalization of abortion, admitted to fabricating the myth of the back-alley abortion crisis long ago. "The figure we constantly fed to the media was 10,000 [lives lost to unsafe, illegal abortions each year]," Nathanson wrote. "These false figures took root in the consciousness of Americans, convincing many that we needed to crack the abortion law."[11]

Doctors performed almost all illegal abortions prior to *Roe v. Wade*. But in an ironic twist, the same abortion lobby that rails against back-alley abortions is now pushing to enact legislation that would allow *nondoctors* to perform abortions. California allowed nurse-midwives, physician's assistants, and nurse practitioners to do abortions in 2013.[12] Other states like Maine[13] and Virginia[14] have since enacted similar legislation.

Meanwhile, Planned Parenthood has rolled out a webcam abortion scheme to dispense dangerous RU-486 abortion drug cocktails without conducting a physical exam. The only physician a chemical abortion client sees is on a screen, appearing remotely from miles away. And a new mail-order-abortion pilot program seeks to make Planned Parenthood the Amazon of abortion.

Legal or not, none of this is safe. According to University of Michigan Clinical Associate Professor of Obstetrics and Gynecology Elizabeth Shadigian, one in ten women experiences immediate complications (20 percent of which are life threatening) following an abortion. Complications include infection, hemorrhage, pulmonary or amniotic fluid embolism, injury to the reproductive organs and other internal organs, hospitalization, possible hysterectomy, future premature birth, placenta previa and even death.[15] Jennifer Morbelli,[16] Tonya Reaves,[17] Lakisha Wilson,[18] and many others like them didn't survive their abortion appointments.

Abortion also carries a connection to mental health problems and substance abuse. Even after factoring in numerous demographic considerations, post-abortive women were found to be significantly more likely to face depression, anxiety, suicidal thoughts, and abuse of drugs and/or alcohol.[19] According to research from the *British Journal of Psychiatry,* post-abortive women face an 81 percent increased risk of mental health problems.[20]

None of these facts are taken from religious texts or political talking points. Peer-reviewed medical and social science research provides plenty of evidence on the harms of abortion. In fact, we could spend countless pages here documenting the physical and mental health dangers of abortion or the names of women who died from supposedly safe, legal abortions.

But unless you're carrying this book with you everywhere you go, a long list won't help you defend life when a spontaneous conversation on abortion arises. So, instead of trying to memorize a medical encyclopedia's worth of data, pick one or two statistics from this section of the book, commit them to memory, and be ready to share when you find yourself making the case for life.

Point 3: The Abortion Industry's Agenda Isn't Health Care; It's Promoting an Ideology

Imagine that a devastating natural disaster struck your community. A massive wildfire, an earthquake, a hurricane, flooding, or some other disaster has brought life in your town to a screeching halt. The governor has declared a state of emergency. The National Guard is on the way.

Before you can even begin to pick up the pieces and rebuild, you need to meet your family's most basic needs—safe shelter, bottled water, and a change of clothes. Fortunately, Planned Parenthood is on the scene to provide you with . . .

. . . condoms and free abortions?

Times of crisis reveal true character. While most of the world rises to the challenge in service to their fellow human beings, Planned Parenthood ignores public health, focusing instead on raising money to peddle even more abortion and contraception.

Just days after the Twin Towers fell, Planned Parenthood of New York City responded to the September 11, 2001, terrorist attacks by making its services free.[21] When Hurricane Katrina devastated the Gulf Coast in 2005, Planned Parenthood's answer was to offer evacuees birth control and abortions.[22] After Hurricanes Irma and Maria hit Florida and Puerto Rico more than a decade later, Planned Parenthood decided abortifacient contraception was the answer.[23] Not to be outdone, the Texas-based abortion chain Whole Woman's Health launched a program to provide free abortions for victims of Hurricane Harvey in 2017.[24]

The abortion industry's strange approach to humanitarian relief isn't limited to the United States. The abortion giant also sends "reproductive health services" around the world to address natural disasters—including following Haiti's devastating 2010 earthquake,[25] Mexico's 2017 earthquakes,[26] and Indonesia's 2018 tsunami.[27]

These examples prove that the abortion industry isn't interested in health care. If it was, it would have sent its doctors, clean water, and first-aid kits to disaster survivors instead of peddling contraception and abortion. But as the saying goes, "When your only tool is a hammer, every problem looks like a nail."

Perhaps the most egregious example of Planned Parenthood's disregard for public health was found during the 2020 coronavirus pandemic. When a devastating surge of coronavirus patients overwhelmed hospitals around the world, bringing public health systems to the brink of collapse, the world shut down for months.

While hospitals and clinics across the country ceased providing elective medical procedures to conserve resources for doctors and nurses on the front lines of the pandemic, the abortion industry sued to remain open. Of course, some governors gave Planned Parenthood a pass. Michigan governor and abortion advocate Gretchen Whitmer did not classify abortion as elective, instead describing it as "fundamental" and "life-sustaining."[28]

Even as private industry and governmental agencies partnered to ramp up the supply of personal protective equipment available to front-line medical workers fighting the pandemic, the abortion industry put its own agenda first. Instead of helping to equip those health-care professionals, Planned Parenthood affiliates in California and Pennsylvania launched donation drives for masks, shoe covers, surgical hats, and even hand sanitizer for staff in their own facilities.[29]

The abortion industry's exploitation of disasters around the world is proof positive that abortion isn't a matter of health care; it's a matter of radical ideology.

❧

Dispensing with the notion that abortion is health care can go a long way toward explaining *what it really is*: violence.

What to Say When Abortion Advocates Claim Abortion Is Health Care

1. Health care is healing, not hurting.

2. There's nothing healthy about pitting a woman against her child. Abortion harms them both.

3. If Planned Parenthood really cares about health, it wouldn't use crises and disasters to peddle abortion on survivors.

CHAPTER 6

Rape

*Love can accomplish all things. Things that are most impossible
become easy where love is at work.*
— St. Therese of Lisieux

Rape is the most difficult and emotional part of the abortion debate.

In almost any abortion conversation—at work, around a dinner table, or in politics—rape quickly takes center stage. Abortion advocates use rape to justify *all* abortions. And they've been quite successful convincing politicians, women, pastors, and even people who identify as pro-life to support abortion in the case of rape.

We have found that pro-lifers fear no topic more than rape. Although they are against aborting babies conceived in any situation, they feel ill equipped and uncomfortable defending the pro-life position when abortion supporters present them with "hard cases" (which almost always involve a violent criminal who raped a teenage girl, and she needs legal abortion as an option).

Abortion supporters turn to the rape argument because it puts them in a seemingly perfect position. They portray abortion opponents as siding with rapists against innocent women. Nearly every government in the world has a rape exception because governments never want to be on the side of violent criminals.

Rape cases make up about 1 percent of all abortions each year. However, it would be a mistake to dismiss abortions that follow rape simply because they are relatively rare. If you or a loved one are the victim of sexual assault, that "rare" case means everything to you. A key part of recognizing and defending the dignity of rape victims is protecting them from further violence in the form of abortion.

Remember the following truths when rape comes up in an abortion conversation.

Point 1: Rape Is a Terrible Crime, and the Rapist Is a Criminal

Sometimes pro-life people skip over the crime and harsh reality of rape to start arguing for the humanity of the baby. Remember, though, the woman is a living victim. We need to acknowledge that early in the conversation both in our tone and in our words.

Affirm that the man is the guilty party and should be in the penitentiary. He is the criminal, and the victim is innocent. *She did nothing wrong.* It is critical to say this because sometimes the person defending abortion in cases of rape is a victim of rape herself, and victims sometimes blame themselves.

Clearly pointing out that the guilty party is the rapist (who deserves to go to prison) affirms the tragedy of rape and is a crucial part of the pro-life answer.

Point 2: Abortion Supporters Believe a Heartfelt Myth—Abortion Removes Rape

Abortion supporters genuinely believe that abortion will help rape victims move on with their lives. They see abortion as necessary to give an ounce of consolation to the evil crime that now leaves the victim pregnant against her will. They might view you as disconnected or heartless for not understanding this harsh reality.

Point 3: When It Comes to Rape, Abortion Supporters Will Understandably Argue with Passion and Emotion

When rape and abortion come up, know that abortion supporters will argue passionately and emotionally (most likely as soon as you say that you don't support abortion even in cases of rape). When dramatic statements and accusations about your intentions are made, endure them in loving silence, be kind, and steer the conversation toward the real people involved in the tragedy of rape: the rapist, the victim, and the baby.

The Rapist

Rapists deserve to go to a penitentiary. Or maybe to meet Sonny from *The Godfather*, who smashed his brother-in-law's head with a trashcan lid after he found out the brother-in-law was beating his sister. Obviously, we're not encouraging that, but the scene accurately shows how most people feel about men who abuse women. The point is, no one is on the side of the rapist. Casually skipping over the crime he committed is irresponsible when defending the unborn.

What to say: "The rapist should go to prison."

The Victim

The woman is the victim and our primary focus when discussing rape and abortion. Abortion advocates assume that we couldn't care less about the victims of rape and only care about unborn children. But that's far from the truth. We love rape victims so much we want to give them real options so they don't fall into the temptation to try to correct evil with more evil.

What to say: "The abortion will not remove the pain of the rape."

The Baby

When a woman becomes pregnant after rape, we need to remind abortion supporters that a baby does exist. If the baby didn't exist, abortion would not be an option. Without a baby, there can be no abortion. The question remains, "What do we do with a baby conceived in rape?"

The baby is not responsible and should not be punished for the circumstances of her conception. No child would choose to be conceived in rape.

We do not gradually gain dignity or value during gestation. We're not mutual funds or stocks that get more valuable over time. We come into existence at conception and then grow.

Likewise, our dignity is not based on the circumstances of our conception. If your parents are healthy, Harvard-educated homeowners who conceived you on their honeymoon in Paris, you are not more valuable than someone conceived in an apartment by two people struggling to make ends meet. You're not more valuable than a child conceived in rape.

Scientifically, there is no difference between you and a child conceived in rape. We are all equal in dignity—no matter the circumstances of our conception. Except for rape, we typically have *more* respect for kids who were not conceived in the best of situations but who overcome great odds in life. Except for rape, we seek to protect kids with troubled or abusive backgrounds even more. Except for rape, we never diminish a child's dignity because of her father's crimes. We certainly would not say that she *never should have been born* because of who her father is.

When else do we punish children for their father's sins? When do we hold babies accountable for their dads' behaviors? If an amusement park attendant stopped a pregnant woman from getting on a roller coaster, and she calmly said, "It's OK. My daughter was conceived in rape," would the attendant let her on the ride? Would the bartender serve her ten whiskeys? Would the skydiving company make an exception and let her jump? No.

We treat human beings with more dignity than we sometimes get credit for, but all of that seems to go out the window when someone is discussing rape and abortion. It is supposed to be the no brainer for why abortion is not just needed but good. But in other scenarios we would not look down on someone as a human being if we found out her father was a criminal.

Rape and abortion punish a unique, innocent human being like no other scenario in our culture.

A baby conceived in rape will always live life as a result of that rape. He or she will go to school, play sports, fail, love, struggle, and reach heights and lows no one can or ought to predict upon conception. The road for a baby conceived in rape is a difficult one, but it is hers alone. No criminal, Dad included, can be used to justify denying her of her right to life.

What to say: "The circumstances of our conception do not determine our human dignity. No child should be devalued because of the sins of the father."

⚘

Arguments against abortion in cases of rape make sense, but real human experience is powerful too.

Hundreds of students—half pro-life and half pro-choice—poured into a packed college lecture hall to hear two women speak; both had been raped. One had an abortion, and one placed her baby for adoption. Each shared the horrific experience of rape. Each shared the experience of considering abortion. And each explained the reason for their decision.

Both used logic without much emotion in sharing why they decided to have or not to have an abortion. Most students, even the pro-life students, understood why the rape victim who chose abortion did so. A spirit of compassion, not judgment, was in the room.

The forum seemed to be wrapping up until the woman who chose abortion said, "Now many people encouraged me and supported me in my decision. They understood, and most women told me they would do the same if they were in my position. This is, after all, why we have legal abortion. But no one, including myself, ever considered what would happen after my abortion. No one ever considered that I would be adding an anniversary to my life."

The students homed in on the term *anniversary*.

We have worked with many victims of rape, and all of them remember the date of their rape. They all have an annual anniversary, a reminder of that horrible event. Similarly, we have met thousands of post-abortive women, and almost all of them know the anniversary of their abortion.

The woman who was raped and chose abortion explained that she did not want her baby to remind her of her tragic rape. She wanted the rape in her past. She then passionately explained how the opposite happened. The rape and the abortion became two parallel traumas that feed off each other. She said that her rape anniversary reminded her of her abortion. And her abortion anniversary reminded her of the rape. She was fighting a double battle because of a decision that was supposed to help her move on from this horrific event but instead magnified her pain.

Her testimony ended as she described encountering God and receiving the strength and grace to find hope and healing.

Then, the rape victim who chose life and gave her baby up for adoption spoke. She shared the joy of getting updates on her son from his adoptive parents. She shared how close she came to choosing abortion before deciding she couldn't do it. And she described how every event of her son's life is a testament that the rape does not define her. She said her rape anniversary reminds her that there is always hope after our worst experiences in life.

The students sat in silence and listened to these two women share the reality of the consequences of rape and abortion. There is no sugarcoating the tragedy of rape or abortion. But a tragedy does not have the ultimate power to change our nature: that we are hardwired to protect our children. Their courage to share their real-life experiences is too often absent from the discussion on rape and abortion. No one thinks about the two anniversaries feeding—positively or negatively—off each other.

These two women's experiences illuminate the victims in this story and demonstrate why abortion can never comfort, console, or solve a woman's problem.

Now let's look at the experience of the child.

⁂

The Planned Parenthood staff gathered outside to hear the speakers at a pro-life event on the sidewalk in front of their workplace the day of the *Roe v. Wade* Supreme Court anniversary.

The last speaker was a young woman in her early twenties. She shared how she was conceived by the act of a criminal when her mother was raped at fourteen. Her father was incarcerated. After nearly deciding to have an abortion, the teenage mom instead gave her daughter up for adoption. More than two decades later, the young woman who nearly lost her life to abortion conveyed the immense gratitude she had for her mom choosing adoption and expressed her love for her adoptive parents.

"Something in my life never changed since the day my mom was raped," the young woman said. "From that day on, I am a result of rape. I cannot change that. I was conceived in rape and will be forever a product of rape."

She then turned to the Planned Parenthood workers standing in the parking lot listening attentively. "Do you see me? Do you look at me differently since I told you how I was conceived? I stand here before you still a result of rape just as I was in the womb. Do you believe my life is worth living because every day I live, I do so because of rape? But that rape does not define my dignity or the dignity of any other child who is conceived in rape."

Just like when the powerful testimonies of the rape victims quieted the university lecture hall, silence poured over both the pro-life audience and the Planned Parenthood workers looking on. That young woman's powerful testimony spoke truth that our culture has forgotten. She went on to get married and have children of her own, ensuring that the impact of her mother's courageous decision to choose life is generational.

❧

Once we know how to effectively discuss rape and abortion, all other pro-abortion arguments become easy to counter. We've made these points with thousands of people in diverse scenarios, including abortion workers on the sidewalk, students on college campuses, and even a pro-abortion NBC News reporter who said that she had never heard a pro-life case against abortion in cases of rape that she agreed with until then.

Trust that when we share the truth with love, minds can be illuminated, and hearts can be changed.

What to Say When Rape and Abortion Come Up

1. The rapist should go to prison.

2. Abortion does not remove rape; it adds to the pain.

3. Human dignity is not defined by the circumstances of our conception.

4. In no other scenario do we punish a baby for the crimes of his or her father.

CHAPTER 7

Climate, Population Control, and Abortion

How can there be too many children?
That is like saying there are too many flowers.
— St. Mother Teresa of Calcutta

In 2011, residents of Huanchaco, Peru, reported human bones poking out from the sand dunes near their homes.[1]

The locals alerted archaeologist Gabriel Prieto, who was working nearby. Prieto began digging and unearthed a grisly scene: the bodies of forty-two children, all victims of human sacrifice more than 500 years before. Precise cuts across the victims' sternums suggest that the children's hearts had been carved out of their chests.[2] By the end of the decade, researchers discovered 185 more bodies, making Huanchaco the site of the largest mass sacrifice of children on record.[3]

The ritual slaughter in the Peruvian desert nearly 600 years ago defies imagination. What in the world could drive a community to kill hundreds of its own children at one time?

Blame it on the weather.

Scientists believe warmer temperatures caused by the El Niño weather pattern might have caused flooding and food shortages, leading the Chimú people to take increasingly drastic measures to appease their gods.[4]

Though Huanchaco is the site of the largest-known child sacrifice in history, it's not the only one. Paganism and the ritual killing of children go hand-in-hand, spanning both centuries and continents.

Everything Old Is New Again

At a 2019 CNN town-hall event, US senator and presidential candidate Bernie Sanders made a startling admission. Sanders said that as president he would employ abortion as a tool to fight climate change.

When an audience member asked whether Sanders would make curbing population growth a key feature of his plan to address a "climate catastrophe," he responded:

> "[T]he answer is yes. And the answer has everything to do with the fact that women . . . have a right to control their own bodies and make reproductive decisions. And the Mexico City Agreement, which denies American aid to those organizations around the world that allow women to have abortions or even get involved in birth control . . . is totally absurd. So, I think especially in poor countries around the world where women do not necessarily want to have large numbers of babies, and where they can have the opportunity through birth control to control the number of kids they have, [that's] something I very, very strongly support.[5]

What's shocking isn't so much that Sanders favors abortion as a means of population control. Overpopulation alarmists have advocated for radical—even coercive—depopulation measures for centuries. The shocking part is that Sanders admitted his extremist position *out loud*. His remarks brought fringe population control proposals into the mainstream. No longer were such ideas relegated to out-of-touch, ivory-tower intellectuals in academia. This was a leading candidate to become the president of the United States of America going on national television to declare that the key to ensuring a future of peace, prosperity, and security is killing children.

Sound familiar? Sanders may style himself a progressive, but he embraces the most backward of ancient superstitions: the belief that child sacrifice can change the weather. Share these three facts to demonstrate why we don't need population control to save the planet.

Point 1: The World Is Not Overpopulated

Classical arguments for population control claim that exponential population growth will crowd the earth, straining the planet's ability to feed, clothe, and shelter its inhabitants. The concern was first popularized more than 200 years ago by economist Thomas Malthus, who noted that human population growth was dramatically outpacing growth in food production. Malthus argued that without checks on human reproduction a future of famine and misery was unavoidable.[6]

While Malthus was right about population growth—more than seven times the number of people occupy the planet than when he wrote[7]—the widescale suffering he predicted failed to materialize. Instead, the subsequent two centuries have been marked by an unimaginable increase in standard of living around the world.

Modern hunger and malnutrition are not the result of too many people competing for limited food supplies. According to the United Nations Food and Agricultural Organization and the World Food Programme, there is enough food for everybody to be well fed; the problem is that not everybody can access it.[8] Limiting the world's population growth will do nothing to solve problems with food distribution.[9]

"What did Malthus miss?" asked a Mount St. Mary's University professor of Sociology, Criminal Justice, and Human Services, Dr. Layton Field. "The Industrial Revolution. He didn't and couldn't anticipate that suddenly food production would enable us to provide for a much larger population."[10]

Furthermore, global population growth has leveled off dramatically. In 1960, the average woman gave birth to five living children in her lifetime. By 2017, that number had been cut in half.[11] For now, that's still above the 2.1 children per woman required to achieve a stable population. But the world fertility rate is dropping sharply. "In roughly three decades, the global population will begin to decline," wrote journalist John Ibbitson and political scientist Darrell Bricker. "Once that decline begins, it will never end."[12]

Still, population control advocates point to poverty in major population centers as evidence of unsustainable growth. "Those who say we have too many people on the planet will look at the slums in major cities to say, 'Hey, if we just had fewer people we wouldn't actually have those kinds of conditions in which people are forced to live today,'" Dr. Field said.

But the Population Research Institute notes that urban overcrowding is not the same as overpopulation. Cities are packed because people choose to live there, not because there's nowhere else for them to go.[13] "In reality, we still have massive amounts of space both in our country and across the globe," Dr. Field said. "It's hard to argue we're out of space. In terms of how we distribute ourselves, that's really a political and economic question." Even as population increases, developments in agricultural technology allow farmers to feed the planet on *less* land than in the past.[14]

OK, so we have enough space to shelter the world and enough resources to feed and clothe the world. But what about Bernie Sanders's concern that housing, feeding, and clothing the world will destroy the environment?

The issue is not whether human beings are responsible for global warming. Save that debate for another day. Instead, make it clear that even if you grant the premise that human-induced climate change is a problem, you still don't need to kill children to protect the environment. It's not necessarily true that more people equals more greenhouse gas emissions. Just as crowding in cities has to do more with human decision making than with overpopulation, carbon emissions are a reflection of much more than the number of people on the planet.

Even before the 2020 coronavirus pandemic slowed emissions, the United States was reducing its carbon footprint. With a growing population[15] and a booming economy, energy-related CO_2 emissions in the country dropped by 2.8 percent.[16]

Look at Pittsburgh, the "Steel City." A town that once conjured up images of smoke, soot, and pollution befitting of a Charles Dickens novel is now a clean, cosmopolitan, and economically thriving metropolis.

Just as advancements in agriculture made it possible to feed an exponentially growing population, science-driven development of clean energy (and perhaps eventually large-scale carbon mitigation technologies[17]) can make it possible to address any potential climate crisis without resorting to killing children. Continuing transition from coal to natural gas has helped significantly reduce carbon emissions resulting from electricity production.[18] Similarly, advances in safe nuclear power hold potential to develop affordable green energy.

Point 2: Population Control Is Systemic Racism

"Hey, it would be great if you didn't reproduce!"

It's difficult to imagine a nastier, more belittling insult. But when politicians, bureaucrats, and busybodies from Western countries tell entire nations and cultures that *not* having children will make the world a better place, they're hailed as humanitarians. Bernie Sanders is far from the only national figure who sees getting rid of babies from impoverished countries as the solution to global poverty, a perceived climate crisis, and a host of other social ills.

Leading the way in targeting the developing world's babies is the United Nations. In 2019, the United Nations Population Fund's Nairobi Summit—which branded itself a conference aiming to improve health and education for women and children—instead served to push the liberalization of abortion worldwide. International Planned Parenthood Federation actually used the conference to announce a campaign to liberalize abortion law in twenty countries.[19]

It's time to call out this discriminatory mentality for what it is: systemic racism.

Culture of Life Africa president, author, and filmmaker Obianuju Ekeocha noted that polls show Africans across the continent "hate abortion."[20] That's why, according to the Guttmacher Institute, just four of Africa's fifty-four countries have "relatively liberal abortion laws," and ten ban it altogether.[21]

Population Research Institute President Steven Mosher notes that even in Nigeria, a country with a high maternal mortality rate, fewer than one in five sexually active women uses contraceptives. Contrary to Western assumptions, less than 10 percent of Nigerians said they lack knowledge of or access to contraception. Instead, Nigerian women refuse it because they "want as many children as possible," oppose contraception personally, or have concerns about contraception's negative effects on their bodies.[22]

However, those traditional family values are under attack by foreign governments and nongovernmental organizations seeking to undermine a cultural respect for life, not only in Africa but throughout the developing world.

Ekeocha describes the Western world's push to impose abortion and contraception on Africa as a form of cultural imperialism and neocolonialism. "There is so much pressure," she said. "Many Western organizations coming to African capitals . . . begin to lobby our government even without the people knowing. They go over the heads of the people . . . and they're offering all kinds of things."[23]

What kinds of things? Help battling terrorism, for starters. "The United States actually said it would help Nigeria with [terrorist group] Boko Haram only if we modify our laws concerning homosexuality, family planning, and birth control," said Nigerian Catholic Bishop Emmanuel Badejo. "[A]ll of this is to be imposed on Africa, at whatever cost: we think that it is immoral and that it is unjust." [24]

The Nairobi Summit's outcome statement set a goal of making abortion an essential component of international aid.[25] According to Ekeocha, Western governments and nonprofit organizations alike make development and humanitarian aid contingent on funding contraception.[26] And it's not just African countries in the crosshairs of the population control lobby; Latin American and Asian nations are increasingly under pressure. Even amidst the 2020 coronavirus pandemic, the United Nations made humanitarian aid contingent on the availability of abortion.[27]

Financial incentives to promote a culture of death have proven increasingly effective at undermining traditional family values in developing countries, which "increasingly rubber stamp whatever programming keeps the money flowing," according to Stefano Gennarini, vice president for Legal Studies at the Center for Family and Human Rights.[28]

In many cases, Western neocolonialists don't even hide their imperialistic intentions. Breakthrough Action, a partnership led by the Johns Hopkins Center for Communication Programs, published a document calling for governments, universities, and other organizations to promote "shifts in social and gender norms" to "stimulate demand for F[amily] P[lanning]."[29] The push to export birth control in pro-life countries isn't a response to unmet demand; it's an attempt to create demand by subverting entire cultures.

In any other case, calling for outsiders to enter a country and attack its most cherished cultural practices and beliefs would be decried as racism. Why do contraception and abortion advocates get a pass?

Environmental concerns provide no defense for attempts to depopulate the developing world. Africa is home to more than 17 percent of the global population[30] but accounts for less than 4 percent of the planet's carbon dioxide emissions.[31] In fact, the European Union emits more CO_2 than Africa and Latin America (Mexico, South America, and Central America) *combined*.[32]

Progressives often claim to oppose racism, imperialism, and colonialism. So why are they in favor of imposing an abortion mindset on cultures that find the killing of unborn children unimaginable?

Point 3: Don't Hurt People to Help the Planet

We need to be good stewards of Earth. As Christians, there's no excuse for recklessly desecrating the planet. But you can't protect God's creation by declaring war on its crowning glory—humanity—through abortion and contraception.

"OK, that argument might work for pro-choice Christians," you might say. "But most of the abortion-supporting environmentalists I talk with aren't Christians but are atheists. How do I persuade secular abortion supporters who neither believe in God nor in the human soul?"

Most atheists are philosophical materialists who believe nothing exists except matter. They claim an unborn baby is nothing more than a meaningless collection of carbon-based molecules with no moral significance. As such, secular environmentalists argue that killing unborn babies to protect the environment isn't just acceptable; it's necessary.

There's only one thing missing. While these environmentally minded atheists are quick to write off the value of an unborn child, they never provide a reason for assigning moral value to the environment. Ask them, "Why is a tree in the Amazon Basin worth protecting, but a human being is not? Why does a collection of carbon-based molecules have value in the rain forest but not in the crib?"

It's a question science can't answer.

But religion can. Even if they claim to be atheists, many secular environmentalists are not. They are pantheists and neo-pagans who worship nature instead of God. Some environmentalists even deify the planet, claiming the "inherent rights of Mother Earth are inalienable in that they arise from the same source as existence."[33]

This adoration of creation takes on the trappings of religious devotion, complete with the remission of sin through the purchase of carbon offset credits. Sure, carbon credits are harmless enough, but—as we saw in Peru and at the CNN climate town hall—pagan nature worship leads to the shedding of innocent blood.

Concern for the environment and respect for human life are not mutually exclusive. According to Dr. Field, conversations about the population the earth can sustain and resource allocation are essential "as long as they're centered on the human dignity of the individual. When we stray from that concept of human dignity and the value, the importance of every single person, I think we're missing the main point of the conversation."

Furthermore, curbs on population growth don't ensure environmental sustainability by any measure. With the most draconian population control measures in the world, China remains the planet's most prolific polluter.

Additionally, by combating an overpopulation problem that doesn't exist, environment-minded population-control advocates are unwittingly triggering an *underpopulation* crisis. Dr. Field points to a demography tool known as a population pyramid:

> In a traditional population pyramid, you'd have a large segment of the population under age 15. Then, it tapers off for older ages. Japan's is literally inverted with a relatively small number of young people who are going to have to carry the weight of a rapidly aging Japanese population.
>
> Most of Southeast Asia is facing this. Most of Western Europe. The United States, too, is going to face some really serious questions.
>
> Estimates have the Social Security program running out of money around 2045 because the Baby Boom generation will exhaust the funds while the number of workers paying into the system declines. These changes will necessitate a real conversation about how to adjust our politics, our policy and our economics.

Technology giants Elon Musk and Jack Ma go even further, stating that population *collapse* will be a global crisis in the coming decades.[34] As population growth tapers off, not only will social services, governmental services, and family relationships be strained, but there will also be additional pressure to accept euthanasia as a means of addressing the inverted population pyramid—a recipe for a nightmare.

What to Say When Abortion Is Pitched As a Solution to Overpopulation

1. The world is not overpopulated.

2. Attempts to impose population control measures on the Third World are racist and imperialist.

3. Care for the planet isn't healthy or authentic if it harms the planet's people.

CHAPTER 8

Does Contraception Reduce Abortion?

*I think you must agree that the campaign
for birth control is not merely of eugenic value,
but is practically identical with the final aims of eugenics.*
— Margaret Sanger, founder of Planned Parenthood

Separating the nearly universal use of contraception from the prevalence of abortion is naïve at best and irresponsible at worst. It will also bite you when abortion comes up in conversation because abortion advocates unceasingly, seemingly, pitch contraception as a way to reduce the abortion rate.

Whether you are for contraception or against it, you need to be able to discuss it factually if you want to defend unborn children. But before we get to the facts, we must acknowledge that contraception can be a sticking point, as many pro-life people disagree on the morality of its use.

For nearly two millennia, all Christians were united in opposing contraception. In 1930, the Anglican Church became the first to allow it. From there, other Christian denominations followed. Today, the only Christian denomination to officially oppose artificial contraception is the Catholic Church—though most Catholics ignore this teaching.

But increasing numbers of Christians—Catholic, Orthodox, Protestant, and Evangelical—are rejecting contraception. And religious division over contraception usually places Christians into one of two camps:

1. Those who reject birth control suggest that if God is Lord of our homes, Lord of our finances, and Lord of our lives, shouldn't He also be Lord of our fertility? Does the Bible not consider children to be His greatest blessing? If fertility is a gift from Him, who are we to reject or manipulate it instead of trusting His will?

2. Those who support birth control argue that contraception is a blessing of modern medicine because it allows us to control how many kids we have based on our income, desire, and stage of life. According to this view, there is nothing wrong with using it as we would use any other medication to enhance our lifestyle.

Contraception never fails to come up during a conversation on abortion. Is the abortion industry's argument that birth control reduces abortion accurate? Let's take a look.

❧

Over the past three decades, the abortion rate has dropped by nearly 50 percent. After topping out at more than 1.6 million lives lost to abortion in 1990,[1] the number of US abortions dropped below 1 million for the first time in 2013.[2] By 2017, the number of American babies aborted further dropped to 862,320[3]—the lowest mark since the *Roe v. Wade* Supreme Court decision legalized abortion in all fifty states.

What caused this massive, long-term shift away from abortion?

Pro-life advocates point to a myriad of factors. The development of ultrasound technology provided a window to the womb, demonstrating the humanity of the unborn child. More than 2,750 pregnancy help centers provide free abortion alternatives and have saved countless lives.[4] Meanwhile, state-level abortion restrictions and defunding of abortion have saved numerous babies and closed abortion facilities. And former abortion workers report that when there are pro-life advocates, prayer warriors, 40 Days for Life participants, or sidewalk counselors in front of an abortion facility, the no-show rate for abortion appointments can spike to as high as 75 percent.

Certainly, the tireless and diverse efforts of pro-lifers have borne fruit. But there's another group that claims credit for plummeting abortion numbers: the abortion industry!

If that claim sounds absurd, it's because it is. You'd never listen to the radio and hear a commercial from a car manufacturer advertising the "least popular car in America" or turn on the television and see a mobile phone company boasting that a record number of customers have switched to another carrier. But abortion advocates incredulously congratulate themselves for declining sales of their industry's core product.

The same billion-dollar abortion industry that demands taxpayer-subsidized abortions and profits off abortions all nine months of pregnancy suddenly has an interest in reducing the abortion rate? Hardly.

We should be skeptical of the abortion industry's claim that increased use of birth control will reduce the unintended pregnancy rate and the supposed "need" for abortion. Contraception messaging from a broad coalition of pro-abortion organizations is remarkably consistent:

- *Planned Parenthood:* "[P]olicies that support family planning services and ensure access to contraception . . .

would reduce the number of unintended pregnancies and the need for abortion."[5]

- *The Center for Reproductive Rights:* "[S]afe, effective contraception can substantially reduce the need for abortion."[6]
- *The ACLU:* "[E]liminating the financial barriers to effective contraceptives . . . would decrease the number of unintended pregnancies and reduce the need for abortion."[7]
- *Catholics for a Free Choice:* "Indeed, the country's Planned Parenthood affiliates have prevented more abortions by providing family planning than have groups . . . who remain adamantly opposed to abortion and refuse to support contraception, the best hope for reducing the need for abortion."[8]
- *NARAL:* "Improving access to birth control and providing people with medically accurate information is at the forefront of our efforts to prevent unintended pregnancy and reduce the need for abortion."[9]

These examples are hardly cherry-picked. A Google search for "contraception 'reduce the need for abortion'" returns nearly a million results, including countless links to articles published by pro-abortion advocates, think tanks, and academics.

This coordinated messaging is strategic. The abortion lobby coined the phrase "reduce the need for abortion" to serve two purposes:

1. The word *need* attempts to legitimize abortion by subtly suggesting that abortion isn't an unnecessary and barbaric act of violence. Instead, the slogan suggests abortion access is on par with food, water, shelter, and other basic necessities required for survival.

2. Abortion providers and advocates know that even five decades after its legalization, most people—even many who consider themselves "pro-choice"—remain deeply uneasy about abortion. The notion that the abortion industry is using contraception to sharply reduce the number of abortions helps fence sitters rationalize their support for even the most radical pro-abortion legislation, politicians, and organizations.

Third Way, a "center-left" think tank, admits that a large majority of Americans believes abortion ends a human life.[10] Still, Third Way argues that with a clever marketing strategy, support for abortion can be a political winner.

> We believe that the key to winning the debate over hot-button culture issues is to appeal to the middle by winning what we call "the battle of reasonableness." Our suggested framework is reducing the need for abortion while protecting the right to have one. This framework allows progressives to hold on to pro-choice principles while addressing the moral concerns that the middle has on abortion.[11]

And how does Third Way suggest "reducing the need for abortion"? You guessed it: by increasing "access to birth control for low-income women."[12]

The same messaging strategy has been effective at assuaging the consciences of nominally pro-life but left-leaning Christians. "If Christians are serious about wanting to decrease the number of abortions, then they should be vocal advocates for access to contraception," states a column in *Baptist News Global*.[13]

But like so many abortion industry talking points, the assertion that contraception reduces the number of abortions just isn't true. The evidence shows that contraception actually expands abortion.

Point 1: Many Forms of Contraception Can Actually *Cause* Early Abortions

Birth control can't be a moderate, "reasonable," common-ground way to reduce the number of abortions when many of the most popular methods of contraception can actually cause early-term abortions.

How can that be? Hormonal forms of contraception, including the birth control pill, the patch, the "Morning After Pill/Plan B," hormonal IUDs, and injectable birth control, have three mechanisms to prevent birth:

1. Prevention of ovulation so there is no egg to fertilize
2. Thickening of cervical mucus, making fertilization unlikely even if "breakthrough ovulation" occurs
3. Changing the lining of a woman's uterus so that a newly conceived embryo cannot implant and receive nourishment necessary for survival[14]

The first two mechanisms are truly contraceptive. But the third is abortifacient because it kills a newly conceived human being before he or she can implant safely in the mother's womb. (Non-hormonal IUDs also prevent implantation.[15]) When abortifacient birth control works by preventing implantation, it means a woman has a "silent abortion" before she realizes she has conceived new life. "Every month she continues to take the Pill increases her chances of having her first—or next—silent abortion," wrote evangelical leader and author Randy Alcorn. "She could have one, two, a half dozen or a dozen of these without ever having a clue."[16]

Birth control advocates try to get around this fact by defining pregnancy as beginning not at fertilization when the new life comes into existence but at implantation. "Pregnancy is established only when a fertilized egg has been implanted in the wall of a woman's uterus," says the Guttmacher Institute. "The definition is critical to distinguishing between a contraceptive, which prevents pregnancy, and an abortion, which terminates it."[17]

But pro-lifers don't oppose abortion because it terminates a pregnancy. (After all, labor and delivery terminate a pregnancy too!) Pro-lifers oppose abortion because it kills an innocent human being. The Guttmacher Institute tries to avoid the humanity of a newly conceived embryo by referring to him or her as a "fertilized egg." But there's no such thing as a fertilized egg. Once fertilization takes place, an egg ceases to exist.[18] The term exists only as an unscientific slur used to dehumanize a newly conceived human being.

Point 2: No Evidence Proves Contraception and Access to Contraception Effectively Reduce the Abortion Rate

It's easy to understand why our culture believes that contraception can reduce abortion rates. In theory, contraception would prevent unintended pregnancies and the vast majority of abortions. In practice, the matter isn't that simple.

Analysis from the pro-abortion Guttmacher Institute reveals that a majority of women who have had abortions used some form of birth control *the same month they became pregnant.*[19] More than 90 percent of post-abortive women had used contraception at some point in their lives.[20]

Nor can abortions be blamed on a lack of *access* to birth control. Contraception is ubiquitous in Western society as numerous methods of low-cost birth control are easily available by prescription or over the counter at pharmacies, department stores, and grocery stores. But even in a culture saturated with birth control, hundreds of thousands of children lose their lives every year after being conceived during a month in which their mothers used some form of contraception.

Rachel Jones, the author of the Guttmacher report, shrugged off the shocking number of children aborted by contraception-using women. "No [contraceptive] method—and no user—is perfect,"[21] she wrote. "That half of women were using a contraceptive method does not mean that contraception is ineffective. Rather, it indicates that women and couples are imperfect."[22]

In other words, contraception is no miracle cure for the abortion epidemic after all. To get around this inconvenient fact, abortion advocates have promoted long-acting reversible contraceptives (LARCs) like intrauterine devices (IUDs) and hormonal injections and patches. Because these longer-lasting methods of birth control don't require women to remember to take a daily pill or to have a condom on hand, the risk of user failure is lower—according to contraception supporters.

But Professor Michael New notes that LARCs are unpopular; women discontinue using them at a high rate; and their long-term effects on public health and pregnancy rates have not been studied. "As such, I doubt they are an effective long-term strategy for lowering abortion rates."

New isn't alone in his skepticism. Like the Guttmacher Institute, the United Kingdom's largest abortion provider found that most of its abortion clients had been using at least one method of birth control when they conceived. "When you encourage women to use contraception, you give them the sense that they can control their fertility," said British Pregnancy Advisory Service Chief Executive Ann Furedi. "Our data shows women cannot control their fertility through contraception alone, even when they are using some of the most effective methods."[23]

Point 3: The Contraceptive Mentality Actually Increases Abortion Rates

Research shows that availability of birth control leads to riskier sexual behavior, more unintended pregnancies, and ultimately more lives lost to abortion. A study that appeared in the *Journal of Health Economics* showed that when the UK cut funding for sex education and contraception, a *decrease* in the teen pregnancy rate followed.

"[Risk compensation] is when somebody uses a technology, such as condoms . . . to reduce the risk, but then they . . . actually lose the risk reduction, [because] they take greater sexual risks," said Dr. Edward Green, director of the HIV Prevention Research Project. "A study that was done in Uganda . . . suggests that with intensive promotion of condoms you actually have people increasing the number of sexual partners."[24]

A former "condom and contraceptive social marketer,"[25] Green is not pro-life. He is an ardent supporter of contraception. He simply recognizes that a false sense of security leads people to make different decisions than they would otherwise.

Furedi notes that contraception and abortion are inextricable from each other. "Family planning is contraception and abortion," she said. "Abortion is birth control that women need when their regular method lets them down."[26]

No less an authority than the United States Supreme Court agrees. In 1992, the nation's highest court took a landmark case challenging *Roe v. Wade*. The court upheld *Roe*, keeping abortion legal, in part because Americans

> have organized intimate relationships and made choices that define their views of themselves and their places in society, in reliance on the availability of abortion in the event that contraception should fail. The ability of women to participate equally in the economic and social life of the Nation has been facilitated by their ability to control their reproductive lives.[27]

Abortion advocates hate pro-life arguments that abortion is used as a method of birth control, but the numbers don't lie. The Guttmacher report estimates that mothers who conceived while on the birth control pill in 2014 accounted for more than 116,000 abortions[28]—making abortion following contraceptive-pill failure the sixth leading cause of death in America.[29] Condoms fared even worse, with condom failure associated with more than 224,000 lives lost to abortion[30]—the nation's third leading cause of death in 2014.[31]

❧

While contraception use certainly remains the norm, the number of those who reject—or at least question—the use of birth control is growing. Most of the hundreds of abortion workers we have helped leave the industry have changed their view on contraception based on the damage it causes and the abortions that result from its use and misuse.

The decades-old assumption that contraception is a blessing that reduces abortion is giving way to the evidence, which says the opposite. Furthermore, the contraceptive mentality arises from a big-picture view that is both dangerous and unnatural: an assumption that human beings ought not *want* children. A culture that assumes the noble task of parenthood is something to be avoided is an empty culture.

What to Say When Contraception Comes Up

1. Many forms of contraception can actually *cause* early abortions.

2. There's no evidence that contraception and access to contraception effectively reduce the abortion rate.

3. The contraceptive mentality actually increases abortion rates.

CHAPTER 9

When It Turns Political

It has been said that politics is the second oldest profession.
I have learned that it bears a striking resemblance to the first.
— President Ronald Reagan

Archie Bunker's daughter, Gloria, wisely told her fiancé (Meathead), "Remember, don't talk to Daddy about religion, politics, or anything else."[1]

There's no getting around it: any conversation on abortion will likely turn to religion and politics because to support abortion you must reject science, reason, and God.

In our walk-on-eggshells culture, "identity politics" grows by the day. We are divided and quick to label each other. If you are pro-life, some will immediately hold you personally responsible for every word and deed of every pro-life politician who has ever lived. All in one swipe, you may be blamed for wars, pandemics, putting kids in cages, and being a bigot.

While your pro-life stance might get you labeled a Trump-loving, warmongering, immigrant-hating, misogynistic bigot, few pro-lifers know how abortion came to be politicized.

We've learned that too many politicians think abortion is a religious issue, and too many pastors think it is a political issue. Sometimes, the fear of being labeled "political" or "religious" becomes an excuse to avoid addressing the severity of abortion.

We do not have that luxury; abortion impacts both politics and religion because it involves the very right to live.

The right to life is inalienable and universal. The abortion debate isn't a matter of pro-lifers imposing their religion on the political realm. It's a matter of politicians attacking the most fundamental of human rights—the right that all other rights depend on.

When abortion supporters tell you pro-life activism is political, let them know the history of how abortion came to be a political issue.

⅞

What do Democratic politicians Joe Biden, Bill Clinton, Al Gore, Jesse Jackson, and Ted Kennedy have in common? Each once took a principled stance *against* abortion.

President Biden actually voted for an amendment to overturn *Roe v. Wade.*[2] President Clinton wrote a letter to a pro-life organization stating, "I am opposed to abortion."[3] Vice President Gore wrote about a "deep personal conviction that abortion is wrong."[4] Jackson decried the practice as "black genocide."[5] And Senator Kennedy wrote eloquently that he "[did] not accept abortion as a response to society's problems" while calling on society to "fulfill its responsibility to its children from the very moment of conception."[6]

What happened?

While it's true the conversion gate only swings one way (you don't see any longtime pregnancy help center directors switch sides to work for the abortion industry), there is a singular notable exception: politicians running for president—usually as Democrats.

It wasn't always this way. In fact, with a strong Catholic base, Democrats were initially the more pro-life of the two major political parties.[7] In 1972, at their last national convention before *Roe v. Wade*, Democrats rejected a platform plank asserting a right to abortion.[8]

Four years later, the first presidential election after *Roe v. Wade* pitted then-Governor Jimmy Carter (a Democrat who said he would not have approved of most abortions[9]) against President Gerald Ford (whose opinion of abortion remains unclear). Imagine not knowing a president's position on abortion today!

Regardless of Ford's views, First Lady Betty Ford was pro-abortion.[10] Ford's vice president, Nelson Rockefeller, had enacted a sweeping legalization of abortion as the governor of New York years before *Roe*.[11] A strong majority of the delegates at the 1976 Republican National Convention supported abortion,[12] while more than two-thirds of Republican voters wanted to keep the government out of the abortion controversy.[13]

When the Supreme Court legalized abortion only three years earlier, five of the seven justices who legalized abortion in the *Roe v. Wade* decision were appointed by Republican presidents while one of the two dissenting justices was appointed by a Democrat.

In spite of widespread Republican support for abortion, delegates at the 1976 Republican convention adopted a party platform plank supporting the enactment of a Human Life Amendment that would guarantee unborn children a constitutionally recognized right to life.[14] Why? To poach pro-life Democrats disillusioned a month earlier by their party's adoption of a platform plank opposing the same Human Life Amendment.[15] The Democratic Party's acceptance of abortion created a vacuum for pro-life voters that Ford and the Republicans were happy to fill.

It wasn't only Democratic voters the Republicans were courting. Facing a steep challenge from strongly pro-life

Ronald Reagan at the 1976 nominating convention, Ford allowed the pro-life language to be inserted into the party platform to appease Reagan's pro-life supporters.[16]

The GOP's newfound pro-life stance was supposed to be temporary. Reeling from the Watergate scandal, Republicans hoped the pro-life platform might earn them enough Catholic and Evangelical Christian votes to swing the 1976 election.[17]

Ultimately, Ford and the Republicans failed to keep the White House but succeeded in winning over pro-lifers. The politically convenient alliance between the GOP and pro-life voters proved to endure long beyond the Ford Administration. "The Republican Party's adoption of a pro-life platform plank in 1976 was a catalyst for the party's alliance with conservative evangelicals," said University of West Georgia History Professor Daniel K. Williams. "But no one foresaw this outcome at the time."[18]

That is to say, the Republicans' alliance with the pro-life movement is something of a historical accident. If not for the inclusion of a mild—especially by today's standards—rejection of the Human Life Amendment at the 1976 Democratic National Convention, it's possible that the Republican Party would have a pro-abortion platform today, while the Democrats might very well have developed a pro-life platform.

But however tentative the Democrats' embrace of abortion was in 1976, the political left would marry the abortion lobby in 1980 . . . and renew its vows in 1992 and again in 2012.

Point 1: The Democrats Went All-In for Abortion in 1980

When Carter won the 1976 presidential election, abortion was still a fluid political issue. It would be more than a decade before abortion politics settled into a Left versus Right,

Democrat versus Republican paradigm. Rank-and-file Republicans and Democrats held remarkably similar views on abortion until at least the *late* 1980s.[19]

The anti-Human Life Amendment 1976 Democratic platform at least acknowledged Americans' discomfort with the killing of unborn children: "We fully recognize the religious and ethical nature of the concerns which many Americans have on the subject of abortion," read the abortion plank. "We feel, however, that it is undesirable to attempt to amend the U.S. Constitution to overturn the Supreme Court decision in this area."[20]

Not good. But not exactly a ringing endorsement of abortion either.

So how did abortion turn into the most polarizing partisan debate in American politics? First, the Democrats' rejection of the Human Life Amendment—mild as it was—created an exodus of disaffected pro-life Democrats who fled to the Republican Party. Secondly, many pro-life Catholic Democrats simply surrendered their pro-life convictions, causing pro-life influence to further wane within the party.[21] At the same time, the influence of radical pro-abortion "second-wave" feminists increased on the Left.[22]

Meanwhile, after Carter defeated Ford, Republicans second-guessed their decision to bypass Reagan for their 1976 presidential nomination. Reagan took control of the party, easily defeating then-pro-choice[23] George H. W. Bush in the 1980 Republican primaries.

Reagan became an unlikely champion for the unborn. As governor of California, he had signed the 1967 "Therapeutic Abortion Act"—a bill supposedly designed to decriminalize abortion in rare situations like rape, incest, and cases in which it was believed that pregnancy would endanger the mother's health. He agonized over the decision to sign the bill into law.

Reagan's advisors warned him that vetoing the bill wouldn't make a difference because California's legislature had a pro-abortion supermajority that could enact the abortion law without the governor's signature. Reagan decided he could limit the loss of innocent life more effectively by watering down and signing the bill than by allowing the legislature to enact the law without his influence.[24] "I am satisfied in my own mind we can morally and logically justify liberalized abortions to protect the health of a mother," Reagan said at the time.[25]

It didn't take long for Reagan to regret signing the bill. The legislation's provision allowing abortions to protect a mother's mental health was exploited extensively, resulting in a monumental loss of unborn life.[26] Secretary Bill Clark, who served in the Reagan Administration, described the Therapeutic Abortion Act as "perhaps Reagan's greatest disappointment in public life."[27]

That disappointment transformed Reagan into a staunch pro-lifer. Under his leadership, the 1980 Republican Party platform became more explicitly pro-life. The 1976 platform included a half-sentence endorsement of a Human Life Amendment—but only after a rambling, milquetoast, six-and-a-half-sentence acknowledgment that abortion is a "difficult" question that warrants "dialogue."[28] Reagan's 1980 Republicans passed a pro-life plank calling not only for a Human Life Amendment but also for Congressional defunding of abortion and "the appointment of judges at all levels of the judiciary who respect traditional families and the sanctity of innocent human life."[29]

Democrats went in the other direction. Their 1980 platform that defined abortion as a "reproductive right" affirmed the *Roe v. Wade* decision and labeled "reproductive freedom as a fundamental human right."[30] Unlike four years earlier, when Carter tried to assuage Catholic bishops' fears over the

Democrats' pro-abortion platform, no Democratic leader made an effort to meet with the bishops to discuss abortion.[31]

The die had been cast. With its 1980 party platform, the Democratic Party hitched its wagon to the abortion industry.

Point 2: Clinton Called for Abortion to Be "Safe, Legal, and Rare," but the Party Purged the Pro-Life Viewpoint

As Democrats coalesced in favor of abortion throughout the 1980s, any misgivings over the legality of abortion evaporated. In 1988, conciliatory language recognizing pro-life concerns about abortion disappeared from the party platform[32]—replaced in 1992 by demands for a federal law guaranteeing a right to abortion on demand, "regardless of ability to pay."[33]

With their party thoroughly wedded to the abortion lobby, Democratic politicians with aspirations of holding national office began abandoning previously held pro-life principles. The reversal was awkward. It wasn't hard for Republicans like Reagan and Bush to justify their pro-life evolution to supporters, who saw the conversions as sincere.[34] But newly pro-choice politicians struggled to explain their sudden support for dismembering unborn children after years of acknowledging the brutality of abortion.

"Democrats tripped over themselves trying to appear both for and against abortion," wrote *The Atlantic* author Caitlin Flanagan. "While Jimmy Carter, [1984 nominee] Walter Mondale, and [1988 nominee] Michael Dukakis all supported legal abortion, they also expressed their personal distaste for the procedure . . . . [After 12 years of pro-life presidents,] Democrats were eager for a candidate who was an adamant and unembarrassed supporter of abortion rights."[35]

Like Carter, Mondale, and Dukakis, 1992 nominee Bill Clinton had also sent mixed messages on abortion. But unlike that trio of failed nominees, Clinton had the political skill to transform his past waffling into a strength.[36] By calling for abortion to be, "safe, legal, and rare," Clinton seemingly managed to find common ground between abortion supporters and opponents, reconciling concern for women's rights and concern for the lives of unborn babies.

Shouldn't abortion be safe? Nobody—pro-life or pro-choice—favors unsafe abortions.

Why not keep abortion legal so that desperate young mothers aren't dragged off to prison after having abortions?

And who doesn't want abortion to be rare? Nobody *wants* to have an abortion.

Clinton's "safe, legal, and rare" mantra sounds like a brilliant approach to the world's most controversial subject—as long as you don't examine the slogan too closely. After all:

- How can a surgery that intentionally kills an innocent human being ever be considered safe?
- Why should killing an innocent human being be legal? (Though the abortion industry mongered fears of post-abortive women being dragged off to prison, the pro-life movement has long recognized women as *victims* of abortion and sought to punish doctors who perform abortions—not the women who procure them.)
- And why in the world was Clinton talking about abortion being rare? (Abortion numbers peaked in the early 1990s when abortion—the most common surgical procedure in the country—claimed more than 1.5 million lives a year.[37])

Clinton's position on abortion was so extreme that he *twice* vetoed legislation banning the dismemberment of children *during* birth.[38] But his "safe, legal, and rare" slogan cleverly provided a fig leaf to voters looking for a way to support a candidate in favor of killing defenseless children.

Clinton's savvy rhetoric soothed the consciences of moderate and undecided voters, but Democrats were not as patient with their own elected officials. A long line of Democratic politicians migrated from the pro-life position to a Planned Parenthood endorsement. However, when Pennsylvania governor Bob Casey stayed true to his pro-life convictions, he paid a price.

Casey requested an opportunity to present a "minority report" opposing the increasingly pro-abortion party platform at the 1992 Democratic National Convention. "All I wanted was a chance to speak to offer a strong dissent based on the party's historic commitment to protecting the powerless," Casey wrote.[39]

Democratic leadership refused.[40]

It's not that Casey was a menace to the party, a squishy moderate, or a "Democrat in Name Only." He was a liberal who advocated for universal health insurance, labor unions, increased public school funding, recycling, and even a tax increase.[41] And he had just won a landslide reelection as the governor of the country's fifth most populous state—more than doubling the vote total of his opponent.[42]

Normally, that type of résumé would wield considerable influence among party leadership. But Casey's opposition to abortion rendered him a persona non grata. *New York Times* religion writer Peter Steinfels described the rejection as a "watershed" moment: "At the national level of one of the two major political parties, opposition to abortion had become literally unspeakable."[43]

Point 3: 2012 Marked a Turning Point As "Safe, Legal, and Rare" Became Legal, On-Demand, and Taxpayer Funded

Eight years after her tenure as first lady ended, Secretary of State Hillary Clinton sought to return to the White House as president. Campaigning to become the Democratic nominee, Clinton tried to recreate her husband's all-things-to-all people approach on abortion. "I believe abortion should be safe, legal and rare," she said—adding for good measure, "and when I say 'rare,' I mean rare!"[44]

But Secretary Clinton couldn't recreate President Clinton's political alchemy selling abortion to a polarized electorate. The abortion industry had long since solidified its hold on the Democratic Party, and abortion advocates weren't exactly enthusiastic about the suggestion that abortion should be rare. The abortion lobby complained that the "safe, legal, and rare" slogan stigmatizes abortion.[45] According to Destiny Lopez, co-director of a pro-abortion special-interest group, instead of making abortion "rare," it should be made "accessible and affordable."[46]

Clinton lost the 2008 nomination to Barack Obama, who had no intention of making abortion rare. Instead, Obama pledged that his first act as president would be to sign a law overturning *all* pro-life laws and regulations.[47] With Obama running for reelection in 2012, the Democratic Party again rewrote its platform's abortion plank.

Twenty years after Bill Clinton coined the phrase "safe, legal, and rare," his party dropped the call for abortion to be "rare."[48] In doing so, Democrats concluded a forty-year journey. Only four decades after overwhelmingly rejecting a pro-abortion platform, Democrats wouldn't so much as suggest abortion is less than ideal. Hillary Clinton learned her lesson. She, too, quit saying abortion should be rare when she ran for president again in 2016.[49]

Unable to even concede that there's *anything* wrong with abortion, the Democrats have since abandoned all restraint in their enthusiasm for abortion. The party's 2016 platform called for

- direct taxpayer funding for abortion—a position taken by now-President Joe Biden (after suddenly reversing his early opposition to public abortion funding) and every other Democrat who ran for president in 2020[50]
- a repeal of all federal and state abortion restrictions[51]
- a declaration that the right to abortion is "unequivocal"[52]

Democrats doubled down on abortion expansion yet again in their 2020 platform, adding demands for

- expanded delivery of abortion pills (which are often distributed without an abortion client ever being examined by a doctor)
- funding for abortion in developing countries
- population control
- eliminating conscience protections for health care providers[53]

The outlook for pro-life Democrats going forward is grim as the Democratic caucus has been nearly entirely purged of pro-lifers.[54] The party of the "little guy" is waging total war on the littlest of guys.

❦

After fifty years of abortion battles in Washington, DC, the lesson is clear. Yes, we need to elect righteous men and women to enact just laws that reflect the natural moral law God established. But politicians are fickle.

Of the eight Republicans nominated for president since *Roe v. Wade*, three used to be pro-choice (Donald Trump, Mitt Romney, and George H. W. Bush). Three used abortion as a political pawn, emphasizing and deemphasizing their pro-life convictions depending on how they felt it would impact their electoral prospects (John McCain, Bob Dole, and Gerald Ford). And Reagan became a pro-life stalwart only after signing (however reluctantly) landmark legislation dramatically expanding abortion in California.

Of the nine Democratic presidential nominees, three (Biden, Gore, and Bill Clinton) dramatically liberalized their position on abortion prior to running for president, while four (Hillary Clinton,[55] Dukakis, Mondale, and Carter) expressed a personal opposition to abortion—and used their political power to expand it.

What to Say Regarding Politics and Abortion

1. Politicians from both parties have flip-flopped on abortion.

2. In 1980, Democrats committed to supporting abortion in their party platform.

3. In 1992 (and while preaching that abortion should be "rare"), Democrats silenced a popular and accomplished pro-life governor from speaking at their national convention.

4. In 2012, Democrats liberalized the abortion plank in their platform again, refusing to even suggest that abortion should be rare.

5. By the 2016 and 2020 elections, Democrats further radical-
   ized, calling for the repeal of federal, state, and local restrictions on abortion.

And then remember that—as important as politics and
voting pro-life are—politicians come and go. Their support
or rejection of abortion would be irrelevant if abortion were
unthinkable and no parents ever considered paying a physician
to end the life of their child. It's not a cliché to say this is ultimately about hearts, minds, and souls; it's reality.

CHAPTER 10

What *They* Say When

I am destroying a life.
— Dr. Benjamin Kalish, abortionist

There is a common—and a little strange—trend in America: when a loved one has surgery, you will hear all about it *in detail.*

Some people love learning the wonders of how modern medicine works and what it can do. Others simply find comfort in knowing that the puncturing, tearing, and violence of Aunt Edna's surgery will leave her healthier and happier than before.

We even like to know a little about the doctor. As Jerry Seinfeld pointed out, everyone thinks their doctor is *the greatest.* "This guy's the best."[1] Seinfeld comically pointed out the impossibility of *everybody* having the number-one doctor. Somebody has to graduate medical school at the bottom of the class.

A little knowledge about one's surgery and the doctor performing it instill confidence in patients and those who care about them. That's another reason—when it comes to surgery—we discuss such personal details openly with family and friends.

But there's one notable exception: the most common surgery in the world—and one that takes place nearly 2,500 times per day in America alone.

Abortion is the one surgery we do not discuss openly. We don't share details or call relatives to inform them about it. We do not care who the doctor is. We might not even know the doctor's name. Most likely, we will not even speak to the doctor other than a simple greeting. There is no bragging about his previous surgeries or medical accomplishments. Most likely, he doesn't even live in our community.

Abortion is the complete opposite of any other surgery. It does not tear, dismember, or cut to heal but to kill. Abortion does not exist to enhance, prolong, or restore life but to end it.

We can make many points to oppose abortion.

Sometimes, however, the most effective arguments against abortion come from abortion doctors and abortion supporters themselves. (The powerful testimonies of former abortion doctors and abortion workers who now oppose abortion could fill volumes. We quote them often.) But these former abortion workers are often dismissed and disregarded as disgruntled employees or fanatics who "got religion."

Abortion doctors do not live in a fantasy world. Many abortion industry insiders' public remarks show that they are literally trying to play God—and they know it. Nothing makes the pro-life case more powerfully and more irrefutably than the words of the doctors who do abortions and the executives who market them. These comments cut through all the Madison Avenue marketing phrases that cloud abortion in slogan and euphemism.

Abortion providers and executives' own words prove that abortion exists to kill a baby. The quotations here (with a few exceptions) come from active and unrepentant abortion doctors and abortion workers.

"Women are not stupid . . . . Women have always known that there was a life there."[2]
   —*Faye Wattleton, former president of Planned Parenthood*

"Currently, the violence and, frankly, the gruesomeness of abortion is owned only by those who would like to see abortion (at any time in pregnancy) disappear . . . . The pro-choice movement has not owned or owned up to the reality of the fetus, or the reality of fetal parts. Since the common anti-abortion stance is that the fetus has a right to life, those who support abortion access necessarily deny such a right. However, in doing so, the fetus is usually neglected entirely, becomes unimportant, nothing. . . . Of course, acknowledging the violence of abortion risks admitting that the stereotypes that anti-abortion forces hold of us are true—that we are butchers, etc. It is worth considering for a moment the relationship of feminism to violence. In general feminism is a peaceful movement. It does not condone violent problem-solving and opposes war and capital punishment. But abortion is a version of violence. What do we do with that contradiction?"[3]
   —*Dr. Lisa Harris*

"Life begins at conception and what I do is murder. . . . Clinic workers may say they support a woman's right to choose, but they will also say that they do not want to see tiny hands and tiny feet. There is a great difference between the intellectual support of a woman's right to choose and the actual participation in the carnage of abortion. Because seeing body parts bothers the workers."[4]
   —*Judith Fetrow, Planned Parenthood worker (Judith worked as an abortion counselor and as a surgical assistant during abortion procedures.)*

*Late term abortionist **Dr. Leroy Carhart**,* who does abortions through the third trimester, told reporter Hilary Andersson of the BBC that he believes he is killing babies. Here is part of the transcript:

Hilary Andersson: "It's interesting you use the word *baby*, because most abortionists won't use that—they'll use the word *fetus*, because they don't want to acknowledge—"

Carhart: "I think that it is a baby, and I use [the word] with patients. To the fetus it makes no difference whether it's born or not born. The baby has no input in this as far as I'm concerned."

Hilary Andersson: "And you don't have a problem . . . with . . . killing a baby?"

Carhart: "I have no problem if it's in the mother's uterus."[5]

"I feel that abortion involves taking a human life, irrespective of the gestation. I feel that there are circumstances where it is clearly inhumane to ask a woman to carry on with the pregnancy, for example, if child abuse or rape had occurred. Having decided that taking a life by abortion is sometimes the lesser evil, I do not feel able to judge between one woman's need and another—this would be completely unacceptable ethically. I would also find it personally difficult to wash my hands of a woman wanting abortion just in order to protect my own moral purity. I will therefore do any abortion at any gestation if the woman is sure herself that abortion is her only option. I think that I would not find an abortion possible for myself and would not have antenatal screening for fetal abnormality."[6]

—*Joanna Brien and Ida Fairbairn, Pregnancy and Abortion Counseling*

"I am 77 years young, and my heart and its valves have been working nonstop since my days as an embryo in my mother's uterus."[7]
—*Dr. Bruce Steir*

"Abortion is life and death, and I think for me it's about providers saying, 'Yes, we end lives here,' and being okay with that. . . . I had a woman wake up in the recovery room and say, 'I just killed my baby.' And I said to her, 'You did, and that's okay.' And just, being okay, to say that. . . . That's what I feel we're doing here. And I'm okay with that."[8]
—*Dr. Jeanne St. Amour*

"The abortion clinics have become the new Cathedrals of our age—its workers, the grassroots clergy. Here, there is existential dread, anxiety, an initial taste of power . . . the crushing fundamental truth coming home that you are responsible for your own life and the life growing inside you."[9]
—*Merle Hoffman, abortion facility owner*

"I have angry feelings at myself for feeling good about grasping the calvaria [head], for feeling good about doing a technically good procedure that destroys a fetus, kills a baby."[10]
—*Dr. Diane M. Gianelli*

"It is morally and ethically wrong to do abortions without acknowledging what it means to do them. I performed abortions, I have had an abortion, and I am in favor of women having abortions when we choose to do so. But we should never disregard the fact that being pregnant means there is a baby growing inside of a woman, a baby whose life is ended. We ought not to pretend this is not happening."[11]
—*Dr. Judith Arcana*

"Abortions are very draining, exhausting, and heartrending. There are a lot of tears. . . . I do them because I take the attitude that women are going to terminate babies and deserve the same kind of treatment as women who carry babies . . . . I've done a couple thousand, and it turned into a significant financial boon, but I also feel I've provided an important service. The only way I can do an abortion is to consider only the woman as my patient and block out the baby."[12]
 —*Dr. John Pekkanen*

"No one, neither the patient receiving the abortion, nor the person doing the abortion, is ever, at any time, unaware that they are ending a life."[13]
 —*Dr. William Harrison*

"Abortion is killing the fetus. . . . Human life, in and of itself, is not sacred. Human life, per se, is not inviolate."[14]
 —*Anonymous abortion doctor, Boston Magazine*

"Dr. William Rashbaum performed thousands of abortions before his death in 2005. He revealed to an interviewer that he was haunted by a recurring nightmare of an unborn baby hanging on to the uterine wall with its tiny fingernails, fighting to stay inside. When asked how he dealt with this dream, he said, 'Learned to live with it. Like people in concentration camps.'"[15]

"It [abortion] goes against all things which are natural. It's a termination of a life, however you look at it."[16]
 —*Dr. Miriam Claire*

"So, it's like putting meat in a Crock-pot, OK, it doesn't get, it doesn't get broke, but it just gets softer."[17]
 —*Dr. Leroy Carhart*

❧

Abortion is unlike any other surgery, and abortionists are unlike any other doctor. No wonder there is a shortage of them. This is the only surgery we avoid describing, and they are the only doctors we don't want to know—even if we are their patients.

Quoting abortion doctors about the work they do illustrates the mentality of those who carry out abortions on a daily basis—and holds abortion advocates accountable for the violence they support.

What to Say about Abortion Using the Words of Abortion Doctors, Executives, and Promoters Themselves

1. Use abortionists' graphic descriptions to show abortion for what it truly is: violence.

2. Point out that nobody knows more about abortion or supports abortion more than the abortion doctors and workers you're quoting.

CHAPTER 11

IVF, Surrogacy, and Other Artificial Reproductive Technologies

*We don't know what we're doing
because we don't know what we're undoing.*
— G. K. Chesterton

The desire to have children is ingrained in the human heart. Children require much sacrifice and much love, and no job on Earth is more important or rewarding job than rearing children.

Conversations on abortion often turn to artificial reproductive technologies. We both have loved ones who have used technologies like in vitro fertilization (IVF), surrogacy, and other artificial means to bring a life into the world after desperately trying to have a baby naturally.

Many people who oppose abortion from the moment of conception—even in the most difficult cases—celebrate artificial reproduction as a blessing, a gift from God. Technologies like IVF and surrogacy would *seem* to be the *exact opposite* of abortion because they offer infertile couples who desperately want a child real hope of becoming parents. That must be a good thing, right? Utilizing modern technology to welcome more babies into the world sure sounds pro-life.

For pro-lifers to defend each and every human life as the priceless image of Almighty God and then deny infertile couples the opportunity to bring children into the world through the wonders of modern technology can appear hypocritical and cruel. Communicating why must be done gently and compassionately. Here's what to say when artificial reproductive technologies come up in conversation.

Point 1: Artificial Reproductive Technologies Destroy and Dehumanize Newly Created Children

For every child successfully brought to birth through an IVF treatment, many more typically lose their lives during the process.

A typical IVF cycle might create eight human embryos.[1] Of those eight human lives, it's likely only one or two will survive to birth. What happens to the rest?

Newly created embryos spend their first five to six days growing in a laboratory. At least half (and as many as 70 percent) of those embryos die by day 6.[2] Once an embryo is transferred to the mother, the likelihood of the child being lost to an ectopic pregnancy (a condition that is also dangerous for the mother) doubles or triples.[3] Only about a third of IVF cycles result in a live birth, meaning the most likely outcome of a single cycle is that all eight embryos die.[4]

Even if a child does make it through the process to birth, perinatal outcomes are still significantly worse for babies conceived using IVF compared with naturally conceived babies.[5]

IVF is expensive, with conservative estimates putting the cost at around $20,000 per cycle.[6] With nearly two-thirds of IVF cycles failing to bring a child to birth, a family can easily rack up many tens of thousands of dollars in medical bills. Of course, anyone desperate for a child would pay that amount and more to have a child, but no one would do it at the expense of their other children.

The high cost of IVF leads many IVF clients to "hedge their bets" by creating more embryos than necessary. For example, of the eight embryos created, as many as four will survive to day 6. But the IVF doctor might transfer only one or two to the mother's womb.

Again, what happens with the rest?

Some are frozen to be saved for later. Because storage fees for frozen embryos can exceed $1,000 a year, many are abandoned.[7] Some are destroyed and discarded. Some are given to other infertile couples. And the rest are killed so their tissue can be harvested for research purposes.[8]

These are unique, individual human beings we're talking about.

Dr. Craig Sweet said that more than one in every five embryos he has created via IVF have been abandoned. "We weren't prepared for any of this," he admitted.[9]

Because fertility clinics are not required to disclose how many frozen embryos they store, nobody knows how many tiny, frozen people live in a sort of suspended animation in laboratories across America. One study suggested the number could be as high as 1.4 million.[10] If all those embryos were gathered into one place, it would become the eighth most populous city in the country, between San Antonio and San Diego.[11]

Not only do IVF doctors create more embryos than might be necessary. They often play the odds by implanting multiple embryos into a mother's womb during a single cycle—aware that some of them might not survive pregnancy.

But sometimes most or all those embryos do successfully implant. If a mother is pregnant with triplets, quadruplets, quintuplets, or even more babies, IVF doctors often advise a "multifetal pregnancy reduction" or "selective reduction" where an abortion doctor uses an ultrasound to kill all but one or two of the unborn babies.[12] These abortions sometimes go wrong, killing all the babies involved.[13]

Bearing too many babies isn't the only reason some of the created embryos are willingly destroyed. Many parents pursuing IVF screen their children—both before and after implantation—so that any children with disabilities or genetic abnormalities can be destroyed before birth.

In the case of gestational surrogacy (where a mother carries another couple's child), the parents who commission the surrogate mother can contractually require her to have an abortion if the unborn child is diagnosed with any health problems or genetic anomalies.

These abortion clauses aren't hidden in the fine print. They're a basic part of negotiations for all couples who choose surrogacy.

One of the leading surrogacy websites, Surrogate.com, states, "In many surrogacy journeys, any decisions regarding pregnancy termination or selective reduction fall to the intended parents. This is understandable; while the gestational surrogate is the one carrying the pregnancy, the intended parents are the ones who will take custody and responsibility of any children resulting from the surrogacy."[14]

Still, abortion clauses have led to many lawsuits. In 2016, a surrogate mother refused abortion and was sued by the father who "threatened to financially ruin the 47-year-old surrogate mom by imposing monetary damages if she refused to abort one of the fetuses, citing a provision in their contract that allowed him to request a 'reduction.'"[15]

In Connecticut, a couple found out their baby (who was growing in a surrogate mother) had disabilities. They decided they didn't want the baby anymore, so they insisted the surrogate mother have an abortion. When the surrogate mother refused, the couple offered her $10,000 to abort their own baby. The surrogate mother refused, and they ended up in a legal standoff to try to force the surrogate mother to have an abortion.[16]

Point 2: Artificial Reproductive Technologies Exploit Women and Children

Billions of dollars change hands each year through the US fertility market. The majority of fertility industry revenue is driven by artificial reproduction.[17]

At best, these technologies are exploitative. At worst, they involve human trafficking.

That's not hyperbole. Children created by artificial reproductive technologies literally become property. Amidst a high-profile custody battle over a client's unused embryos, one attorney issued a statement illustrating the cold commodification of IVF: "That genetic material [four frozen children] was created pursuant to a written agreement that required both parties' written consent to attempt to create a pregnancy."[18]

The biomedical research industry has also turned artificially conceived children into property. More than 1,000 patents have been issued for cell lines derived from babies conceived in fertility clinics—and later destroyed for research purposes.[19]

The exploitation of artificially created children is built into the very language of the industry. Websites marketing artificial reproduction to prospective clients discuss how many embryos to "use" and what to do with "unused" embryos.

Children are not meant to be used or put through some brave new world experiment that is held together by financial contracts and court documents. Children deserve to be loved for their own sake. But artificial reproduction values children not for their inherent worth but as products to be acquired. That's why women who sell their eggs can command top dollar if they have the "right" physical features, ethnicity, and even SAT scores.[20]

Ultimately, science unconstrained by ethics tempts parents to build their children to specification. It's not only a matter of genetic screening either. New gene-editing technology offers the potential for parents to literally custom-make children free from health conditions that might cause suffering.

And that's just the start. Wide-eyed journalists imagine genetically engineering babies to be stronger and smarter as they envision "taking a much more active . . . hand in shaping the evolution of the human species."[21] This Utopian vision values people not for *who they are* but for *what they do*. It's a recipe for mass carnage. The tough and tender-hearted use of eugenics to reengineer human nature and build a better society has been tried and always leads to the destruction of human life.

Respect for human dignity also means that children deserve to be conceived and born in the context of marriage. They deserve to be created in a loving embrace rather than in a test tube. They deserve to have a mother and a father rather than some conglomeration of biological, gestational, and commissioning parents whom they might never meet.

"I hate being donor-conceived," wrote one person conceived via artificial reproduction. "I think it is ridiculous and bizarre that the two people that made me have never met and never will meet. I think it's creepy that my dad was paid."[22]

While many children conceived through artificial reproduction are concerned about the family members they'll never meet, others have to worry about the relatives they might meet—and *date*.

"When you're dating, you'll have to be careful," Julia Berman's mother warned her when she was only seven years old. "And take a DNA test to make sure it's not your half sibling."

Berman has thirty-two half-brothers and half-sisters—all conceived with sperm from the same donor.[23]

While artificial reproduction is an inherently immoral process, we must be careful not to further dehumanize children conceived artificially with our rhetoric. Many of them will struggle with self-identity issues. We can be bold *and* sensitive as we oppose artificial reproduction while simultaneously affirming the innate dignity of every child conceived artificially.

Children aren't the only people exploited by artificial reproduction. The industry also takes advantage of desperate women—many in impoverished, developing countries—who sell their eggs or rent out their wombs as surrogate mothers. All for the benefit of those who can afford six-figure payouts to outsource pregnancy.

Little is known about the health impact on the women selling eggs or carrying children by contract. Women who sell their eggs need numerous hormone injections, and there is little research on the long-term effects of the process.[24]

"Surrogacy was a bazaar where everything about women's reproductive capacity and the children born was priced," wrote Dr. Sheela Saravanan in a book examining the fertility industry's exploitation of women in India.[25]

"Wealthy people want children, so they hire scientists to make them, and then pay poor women to carry and bear them," wrote Rachel Lu in *National Review*.[26]

"There are issues of class exploitation here," said Jennifer Lahl, president of the Center for Bioethics and Culture Network. "Have you seen a tabloid magazine that features a wealthy Hollywood celebrity serving as a surrogate for her poor housekeeper?"[27]

Lu goes even further, arguing that surrogate mothers and those who sell their eggs are not the only women degraded by artificial reproduction. *All* mothers are, she says. Surrogacy, in particular, reduces motherhood to one more form of labor that can be priced by the market. "To avoid the charge that they are selling babies, proponents of surrogacy must contend that pregnancy and birth are properly seen as a job, of a sort that can be outsourced."[28]

Many women who agree to become surrogate mothers essentially sell themselves into slavery. "I've read many, many surrogacy contracts, and they control, in detail, every aspect of the woman's life, from before conception and embryo transfer, through the birth, and even after, if she's also being contracted to provide breast milk," Lahl said.[29]

The surrogacy mentality is a frontal attack on the very nature of the family. If the job of bearing children can be outsourced with a simple employment contract, there's nothing particularly special about the relationship among a mother, a father, and a child. The deliberate erosion of family relationships and parental rights weakens the family against the coercive power of the government.[30]

Point 3: For Treating Infertility, More Ethical, Affordable, and Effective Options Exist Than Artificial Reproduction

Infertility is a cross.

- "Relax. Give it time; it will happen."
- "Have you tried giving up sugar/gluten/red meat?"
- "If you trust God, He will reward your faith."
- "I know you'll be blessed with a child if you are patient."
- "Try this vitamin supplement. It worked for my cousin!"
- "My sister was infertile, and now she has eight babies."

Well-meaning loved ones often try to encourage couples suffering from infertility with advice or even assurances that eventually they'll welcome a child into the world.

Sometimes that is the case. We know one woman who was blessed with her first baby two decades into her marriage and another whose doctor solved her fertility problems after more than half a dozen miscarriages. Stories like these are plentiful and provide hope for those longing to become parents.

But infertility is not a *Hallmark* movie. There's no recipe that can guarantee anyone a baby.

We need to be careful about how we encourage infertile couples. Because our reproductive capacity is stamped onto our very bodies, the pain of infertility can feel like a wound to one's identity as a woman or as a man. To suggest that simply relaxing, changing one's diet, or having greater faith can magically result in a healthy baby is to tacitly blame the couple for doing something *wrong*. Many attempts to encourage a couple might actually be *discouraging*.

Instead of making promises, we need to acknowledge the pain of infertility. "I'm so sorry it hasn't happened yet. I love you, and I'm praying for you every day," provides much more comfort and consolation than a saccharine attempt to *solve* your loved one's infertility.

In short, your loved ones suffering infertility need your friendship *more* than they need your advice.

But when they do want advice, offer it tactfully and respectfully—and only if you know what you're talking about. (A tip you saw on Facebook or advice from Oprah most assuredly does not count.) It's a good idea to brush up on ethical alternatives to artificial reproduction like NaProTECHNOLOGY. Short for "natural procreative technology," NaProTECH-NOLOGY charts symptoms from a woman's reproductive cycle to diagnose and treat infertility (and a wide variety of other gynecological health conditions).

Unlike artificial reproductive technologies, NaProTECH-NOLOGY addresses the underlying health conditions that cause infertility. "Most medical approaches today bypass the woman's problem or simply override her natural processes altogether," said NaProTECHNOLOGY pioneer Dr. Thomas Hilgers. "With NaPro, we find out why the body isn't functioning correctly, then apply treatments that work cooperatively with the body."[31]

While a strong majority of IVF cycles fail to result in a live birth, 80 percent of couples using NaProTECHNOLOGY are blessed with a child—many with *no* medical intervention—at a fraction of the cost and with none of the moral and ethical problems of artificial reproduction.[32] One of your authors (Steve Karlen) and his wife used NaProTECHNOLOGY to welcome four more children after years of secondary infertility and miscarriages.

Nothing in life is guaranteed—including the ability to conceive, bear, and deliver life itself. While NaProTECH-NOLOGY can help the majority of infertile couples bring new life into the world, the rest will continue to need your love and your affirmation that they are enough—children or no children.

This is not an easy topic. Only fifty years ago, this chapter could have been viewed as science fiction. But we must address it no matter how difficult it is because it will come up when discussing abortion. Don't shy away from lovingly sharing the consistency of the pro-life message that all human beings have dignity, are unique, and should be protected.

What to Say about In Vitro Fertilization, Surrogacy, and Other Artificial Reproductive Technologies

1. Artificial reproductive technologies bring life into the world at a cost: the destruction and dehumanization of many newly created children.

2. Artificial reproductive technologies exploit women and children, turning them into commodities.

3. Infertility is a cross, but there are more ethical, affordable, and effective options for treating infertility than artificial reproduction.

CHAPTER 12

Planned Parenthood *Is* Abortion

But for my view, I believe that
there should be no more babies.

— Margaret Sanger, founder of Planned Parenthood

Over the summer of 2020, Planned Parenthood's flagship abortion facility in Manhattan found itself desperately in need of rebranding. The abortion empire had long defended its notoriously racist founder. But with America embroiled in a national firestorm over institutionalized racism, it quickly became clear that the Margaret Sanger Planned Parenthood located in Margaret Sanger Square needed a new name.

"The removal of Margaret Sanger's name from our building is both a necessary and overdue step to reckon with our legacy and acknowledge Planned Parenthood's contributions to historical reproductive harm within communities of color," said Planned Parenthood of Greater New York Board Chair Karen Seltzer, who went on to describe Sanger's "racist legacy" as "clearly documented."[1]

Planned Parenthood's admission *sounds* like a step in the right direction, but sadly, it is laughable. Unfortunately, renaming the Manhattan Planned Parenthood center literally proved to be mere window dressing.

Planned Parenthood isn't the first business to check the public relations box by telling the world it doesn't tolerate racism. But its attempt to jump on the anti-racist band-wagon provides remarkable insight into the abortion industry's unshakable foundation. Planned Parenthood dropped Sanger's name, but it continues to carry out everything she believed in to a T—killing children,[2] preying on minorities,[3] and promoting sexual corruption through abortion. Sanger's motives might not be socially acceptable to admit publicly any longer, but by continuing to fulfill her eugenic beliefs, Planned Parenthood's connection to its racist founder and her dilapidated view of humanity is more direct than ever.

Still, many defend the abortion giant and often because of misconceptions. Well-paid public relations professionals in tall buildings have successfully marketed Planned Parenthood not as an abortion provider but as a charitable health-care provider serving those in need. Their efforts have been so effective that a majority of Americans don't even know Planned Parenthood provides abortions.[4]

That means many Planned Parenthood defenders don't actually know what they're defending.

"Planned Parenthood *prevents* abortions," they say.

Or "Planned Parenthood *saves lives* by providing cancer screenings. Why would you be against that?"

Or even "Planned Parenthood helps women *get* pregnant."

Even Americans who do know Planned Parenthood is an abortion provider dramatically underestimate the number of lives the organization takes each year.[5]

But Planned Parenthood *is* abortion. And it's impossible to end abortion without taking on Planned Parenthood. That means we need to cut through the cleverly devised lies about Planned Parenthood and educate our communities that it exists for one reason: to kill unborn children on an industrial scale.

Remember these three facts to explain that *Planned Parenthood IS abortion.*

Point 1: Planned Parenthood Is America's Leading Abortion Provider

Planned Parenthood advocates like to point out that not every Planned Parenthood office does abortions. That's technically true, but every Planned Parenthood office does *sell* abortions. And a robust network of abortion referral satellite clinics helps explain why no organization in America ends the lives of more unborn children than Planned Parenthood.[6] In 2018, the organization killed 345,672 children,[7] placing Planned Parenthood on the list of America's leading causes of death right between cancer and accidents.[8]

The organization operates more than half of America's abortion facilities.[9] And with independent abortion providers going out of business in droves,[10] Planned Parenthood is steadily cornering the market on killing unborn children. Even as the number of abortions in the United States steadily declined over the past three decades,[11] Planned Parenthood has continued to increase the number of abortions it performs each year.[12]

That's not to say Planned Parenthood is in great shape. It, too, is closing facilities. But Planned Parenthood enjoys two key competitive advantages over its independent and small-chain competitors:

1. More than half a billion dollars of taxpayer funding each year.[13] More on that later.
2. The ability to develop new technological methods for widescale delivery of abortion. Just as small businesses

lack the technological infrastructure and complex supply-chain networks to compete with major online and big-box retailers, smaller abortion businesses struggle to keep up with Planned Parenthood.

Planned Parenthood continuously increases its abortion market share by innovating new methods for the delivery of abortion that its competitors simply are unable to match. For example, its telemedicine program dispenses dangerous RU-486 abortion drugs without an abortion client ever receiving a physical exam. The client simply visits her local Planned Parenthood facility and consults with a physician who appears remotely, over a webcam. The woman never actually sees a doctor in person prior to or after her chemical abortion. This reduces staffing costs and overhead compared with independent abortion facilities that require face-to-face doctor visits.

Planned Parenthood is now testing a mail-order-abortion program in seventeen states and Washington, DC.[14] Having already deployed a mobile phone app that allows for mail-order birth control,[15] Planned Parenthood has developed the infrastructure to become the Amazon of abortion.

But what about abortion supporters' claims that abortion comprises only 3 percent of Planned Parenthood's services (now 3 percent according to its annual report)?[16] Planned Parenthood devised the 3 percent figure to minimize the role abortion plays in its mission. But the methods used to come up with these numbers are dishonest. The books are cooked.

Former Planned Parenthood Employee of the Year Abby Johnson has exposed her former employer's accounting "gimmick." Johnson explained that Planned Parenthood "strategically skewed [the three percent figure] by unbundling [non-abortion] services so that each patient shows anywhere from five to 20 'visits' per appointment." In other words, Johnson said, if a woman receives twelve packs of birth control at her appointment, Planned Parenthood counts that appointment as twelve separate client visits.[17]

Johnson said Planned Parenthood then does precisely the opposite for abortion-related appointments. If an abortion requires multiple appointments, Planned Parenthood bundles the appointments together to count as only one visit.[18] So, while a trip to Planned Parenthood for contraception might count for a dozen different services, separate appointments for a pre-abortion consultation, an abortion procedure, and a follow-up appointment (if there is one), only count as one service.

Abortion is Planned Parenthood's core product, and any argument that abortion makes up only 3 percent of its services is as absurd as minimizing the importance of groceries at a supermarket. Sure, you might be able to buy light bulbs, pet supplies, and a magazine while you buy food for your family, but grocery stores are in business to sell groceries. Even Planned Parenthood's former president, Dr. Leana Wen, admitted, "[O]ur core mission is providing, protecting and expanding access to abortion and reproductive health care. We will never back down from that fight."[19] (And Wen was fired for not being sufficiently enthusiastic in prioritizing abortion![20])

A more honest accounting shows that Planned Parenthood performs abortions for approximately 12 percent of its clients annually.[21] There's no sure way to track what percent of Planned Parenthood's pregnant clients receive abortions. But while the organization aborts more than 350,000 babies a year, it provides fewer than 10,000 prenatal services and fewer than 3,000 adoption referrals[22] (which longtime Planned

Parenthood manager Sue Thayer said often consist of nothing more than handing out a brochure on adoption).

Point 2: Any Good Planned Parenthood Does Is Tainted Because It Kills Children

"But what about all the good Planned Parenthood does?" Planned Parenthood supporters respond. The question is, of course, absurd. Don't legitimize it. Instead, remember the context of your conversation. A physician who provides excellent care to some patients and kills others is a *bad* doctor.

Sometimes pro-life people get caught up in discussing "good" things Planned Parenthood does. But would anyone give any credence to arguments defending Hitler for modernizing the jet engine, increasing patriotism, and cutting taxes for the middle class?

An old adage says the first one to bring up Hitler in a debate loses. But while some Jewish people are offended when pro-lifers compare abortion to the Holocaust, other Jewish people are offended when we *don't* bring up the Holocaust. They recognize that we must make a logical but sensitive comparison between the two genocides if we are to stop repeating history's pattern of systematically attacking the dignity of human life.

That said, we are not encouraging you to bring up Hitler at every turn. We're just providing a simple reminder not to give an ounce of credibility to the argument that Planned Parenthood can be justified if it does some good things. Keep this in mind when you are tempted to go point by point into Planned Parenthood's "good" services.

Imagine a daycare center that provides enriching education, healthy snacks, and flexible hours but physically harms some of the children in its care. As a parent, you wouldn't stop to weigh the merits of the string cheese and juice boxes against your concerns about the child abuse. You'd pull your children from the daycare and call the authorities to shut it down because *nothing* can justify harming a child.

The same principle applies to Planned Parenthood and abortion. All the free cancer screenings, free sexually transmitted infection (STI) tests, and free breast exams in the world do not equal the value of one innocent human life. The deliberate killing of a child simply cannot be offset by any other perceived good.

Planned Parenthood advocates object that without the organization, women will lose access to essential health-care services necessary for their long-term wellness—or to save their lives. But when pro-lifers seek to defund and to close Planned Parenthood, we aren't suggesting that legitimate women's health-care services be cut. Instead funding for Planned Parenthood can be redirected toward real health-care providers, like federally qualified health centers (FQHCs), which offer a wider spectrum of health-care services than Planned Parenthood does.[23] Though Planned Parenthood argues that FQHCs would not be able to handle the flood of patients that would result from its defunding, each FQHC would only need to see two more patients per week to fill the gap.[24] And the reallocation of funds formerly designated for Planned Parenthood would make it possible to fund the increased patient load.

Ultimately, Planned Parenthood is an *abortion business*, and its non-abortion services are meant to distract clients, community members, and voters from the barbarity of abortion.

Many of Planned Parenthood's other services are overstated. Some don't even exist. For example, while Planned Parenthood has clamored for taxpayer funding in order to provide women with mammograms, not a single Planned Parenthood facility was certified as a mammography facility.[25] (Conversely, FQHCs provide more than 500,000 mammograms a year.[26])

Planned Parenthood provides less than 1.5 percent of all HIV tests,[27] less than 2 percent of women's cancer screenings,[28] and less than 1 percent of pap tests in America.[29] Provision of services to cancer-screening clients, prenatal clients, and even contraception clients has dropped significantly.[30]

And many of the organization's services (like pregnancy tests and STI tests) are provided not as standalone services but as prerequisites for abortion[31]—meaning Planned Parenthood is not as benevolent as it might appear. A carpenter who gives you a "free" estimate on installing new kitchen cabinets isn't doing so out of the goodness of his heart—but because he's looking to make a sale. When Planned Parenthood administers a pregnancy test, it's looking for a payoff in the form of a $500 abortion.

Point 3: Planned Parenthood Is the Ultimate Evil Special-Interest Group

It would be difficult to imagine a greater villain in American society over the past seventy-five years than the tobacco industry. With a robust marketing strategy that featured celebrity backing, doctor endorsements, and even ads on cartoons, Big Tobacco was everywhere.[32] Its lobbyists wielded considerable influence on elected officials to limit smoking restrictions and regulations.[33] And the industry countered mounting evidence that smoking is dangerous by casting aspersions upon the science[34] as well as by propagating its own bogus research on tobacco's health impact.[35]

The tobacco industry declined throughout the second half of the twentieth century, culminating in a 1998 landmark $206-*billion* settlement to compensate states for smoking-related health-care costs.[36]

Nearly a decade later, US District Judge Gladys Kessler delivered a devastating 1,652-page legal opinion, reading in part, "[Tobacco companies] have marketed and sold their lethal product with zeal, with deception, with a single-minded focus on their financial success, and without regard for the human tragedy or social costs that success exacted."[37]

Sound familiar?

The era of Big Tobacco is over (which proves norms can change quickly), but another special-interest group carries on its legacy of the same business practices, exploitation of children, powerful corporate lobbyists, and reliance on pseudo-science to justify its product: abortion. Of course, the result of an abortion is far worse. Imagine the tobacco companies asking for tax dollars because they serve low-income people who can't bear the thought of not smoking and shouldn't be forced to quit? The messaging is the same: it is their body; it should be their choice.

In the 2019–20 fiscal year, Planned Parenthood raked in more than $600 million of taxpayer funding—nearly 40 percent of its total revenue for the year[38]—even as its legitimate health-care services declined.

That's a lot of cash. How did Planned Parenthood manage to get it? It helps to have friends in high places. The organization likes to portray itself as a charitable public health nonprofit, but Planned Parenthood is a political and legislative powerhouse. In addition to its clinics, the organization also comprises Planned Parenthood Action, a 501(c)(4) lobbying organization,[39] as well as the Planned Parenthood Action Fund

Political Action Committee.[40] The latter committed to pouring $45 million into the 2020 election.[41] It takes money to make money, as the saying goes.

But Planned Parenthood supporters dispute the notion that its lobbyists have secured federal funding for abortion. They argue that a legislative provision called the Hyde Amendment bars public funding of abortion. Instead, they claim that public funding covers Planned Parenthood's *non-abortion* services.

But while taxpayer funding might not pay for abortion procedures directly, it does pay for abortions *indirectly*. Money is fungible and transferable, and federal grants for birth control distribution free up money that can be reallocated for abortion. And even if tax dollars don't cover the actual performance of abortion, those same dollars do cover many of the resources used to perform abortions: medical instruments, staff salaries, the abortion facility building, and more. Furthermore, the Hyde Amendment applies only to the federal government. A number of states do directly fund abortion.

Of course, government handouts aren't the only benefit of being a powerful special-interest group. Planned Parenthood's electioneering influences abortion policy in all three branches of government.

In recent years, abortion industry lobbyists have helped enact sweeping liberalizations of abortion law in states across the country:

- Illinois' Reproductive Health Act *forced* health insurance companies to fund abortion and legalized *partial-birth abortion* while an executive order expanded public funding of abortion.[42]
- Maine enacted legislation that allows non-physicians to perform abortions and mandated public and private health insurance plans to fund abortion.[43]

- New York legalized late-term abortions up to the day of birth and allows non-physicians to perform abortions.[44]
- The "Trust Nevada Women Act" eliminated a requirement that abortion providers inform women about the "emotional implications" of getting an abortion.[45] Supporters of the new law cited studies showing that abortion doesn't result in long-term mental health problems.[46] (Given that numerous studies[47] as well as countless personal testimonies demonstrate the real mental health harm caused by abortion, the abortion industry's favored research is reminiscent of Big Tobacco's "studies" on the dangers of smoking.)

Planned Parenthood lobbyists also prevent the enactment of lifesaving legislation at both the federal and state levels.

Abortion industry electioneering impacts the executive branch, where pro-abortion governors veto pro-life legislation and appoint pro-abortion bureaucrats to administer state policies. At the same time, Planned Parenthood-endorsed attorneys general give Planned Parenthood a pass when it violates the law.

Finally, Planned Parenthood's influence on presidential elections impacts Supreme Court (and other federal court) appointees, who have the power to uphold or strike down pro-life legislation and executive actions.

Our country's most infamous abortion provider, Planned Parenthood is no public-health charity. It's a nefarious special-interest group with an oversized influence on public policy that has resulted in countless deaths.

❦

Proving that Planned Parenthood and abortion are inseparable can go a long way toward winning converts.

What to Say When Planned Parenthood Advocates Try to Justify Their Support

1. Planned Parenthood is America's leading abortion provider.

2. Any good Planned Parenthood does is tainted because it kills children.

3. Planned Parenthood is the ultimate evil special-interest group.

CHAPTER 13

When They Change the Subject

Ignorance is stubborn and prejudice is hard.
— Vice President Adlai Stevenson I

As we've traveled the world and had thousands of conversations about abortion, it is refreshing to continuously rediscover something that should give pro-life people great confidence: most abortion supporters don't actually know much about abortion.

Supporters of abortion fall into three main categories:

1. *The Ignorant:* The majority of abortion supporters fall into this category. They are usually moral relativists who believe offending someone by labeling abortion as wrong is a greater offense than abortion itself. Most are passively pro-choice.

2. *The Deniers:* Abortion advocates who deny fundamental truths about human life and abortion can be easily angered—often as a result of a personal experience with abortion. Be gentle with them, as winning their hearts is more important than winning the argument.

3. *The Eugenicists:* Hard-core abortion industry believers are able to kill without passion. They firmly believe that "might makes right" and that they are serving humankind by cleansing it of "human weeds."[1]

We have helped people from all three categories change their minds and their hearts as they've embraced the pro-life position. No journey is the same. But each of these journeys ends with a firm conviction that abortion is *wrong*. That's why education and outreach are so crucial to the pro-life mission.

Abortion is a simple moral issue. To prove that it's wrong, you only need to demonstrate two propositions, the second of which almost everyone already believes:

1. The embryo or fetus is an innocent human being.
2. There's never a valid reason to end an innocent human being's life.

Convince a person that these two tenets are true, and many will adopt a pro-life stance. But—as with many moral issues—pro-choice people are hesitant to change their minds because they fear that, by standing against an *injustice,* they are standing against *a person.* "But my dear friend had an abortion, and she felt it was her only option," they say. "She's not a villain, and I won't judge her."

To describe abortion as wrong is not to judge those who've had an abortion or even those who do the abortions. It's to speak the truth about what abortion is and what it isn't.

For whatever reason, even after you make a clear and compelling case against abortion, most abortion supporters will double down. Although abortion is a simple moral issue, changing one's mind about it is a much more complicated matter—one with challenging and far-reaching ramifications.

Converting from pro-abortion to pro-life might mean being forced to come to terms with one's own abortion experience. It might require examining one's own political bias. It might result in tense conversations with pro-choice friends and family members.

Changing our minds on important subjects is *uncomfortable* for all of us. So when abortion advocates lose the debate over abortion, many quit talking about abortion and start talking about . . . well . . . everything else!

Don't be surprised when abortion advocates who fail to defend abortion on its own merits try to distract you by raising all sorts of unrelated issues. From immigration policy to personal attacks to truly bizarre philosophical musings, we've heard it all!

Say these three things to return the conversation to the real issue at hand—the violence of abortion.

Point 1: Abortion Is the Preeminent Human-Rights Crisis

One way abortion advocates try to obscure the barbarity of abortion is by reducing it to just one pro-life issue among many. They argue that pro-lifers are insincere unless they take a "seamless garment" approach that places social issues like immigration reform, capital punishment, homelessness, poverty, and the environment on an equal footing with abortion.

It's true that many issues impact and even threaten human life around the world. But as the famous David Allen saying goes, "You can do anything, but you cannot do everything."[2] At least, you can't do everything at the same time.

We can fight abortion *and* homelessness. But when we shoehorn two very different matters into a single issue, we dilute our efforts to solve both problems.

An organization dedicated to feeding the hungry would become considerably less effective at distributing food to those in need if its mission expanded to combating abortion. Similarly, pro-lifers can most effectively serve pregnant moms facing crisis pregnancies and their babies by keeping our mission focused on ending abortion.

Recognizing the rights of the baby in the womb does not require us to turn against anyone else. There is plenty of room in the heart to care about the unborn along with those who suffer from homelessness, AIDS, poverty, or any other form of pain.

All of these concerns are important and worthy of our investment. That's why most pro-lifers' generosity with their time and financial support goes beyond the pro-life movement. Many pro-lifers also serve with other ministries to help provide food, medical care, educational opportunities, and housing to those in need.

Standing against other injustices and working to alleviate other human sufferings stems from a recognition of the pro-life position that life is sacred and, therefore, must be protected.

Every "cause" in our world seeks to make life better for someone else. Every cause assumes that life is good and that it's worth protecting. This belief in the inherent goodness of human life should apply to the unborn as well as to the born.

Even as there are many worthy social-justice movements, two key metrics prove that abortion is the world's preeminent human-rights crisis:

1. *The evil of abortion is categorically greater than the evil involved in other seamless-garment issues.* Tragically, the past century has demonstrated that there is no end to the injustices man is capable of inflicting upon his fellow man. But all of the seamless-garment social-justice issues pale in comparison to abortion:
   - It is wrong to take advantage of the poor for financial gain. But nobody is advocating for killing the poor.

- It is evil to mistreat an immigrant at the national border. But nobody is advocating for slaughtering immigrants on an industrial scale.
- It is immoral to mistreat unskilled workers. But nobody is advocating for murdering unskilled workers.

But half the nation supports killing unborn children—the most defenseless and most innocent members of the human family—on an industrial scale.

And even though capital punishment might be wrong, it is a graver offense to kill one's own baby than to kill a convicted serial killer.

A mother's womb should be the safest place in the world. Abortion has made it the most dangerous.

2. *The tragedy of abortion is on a greater scale than other seamless-garment issues.* This is not to say that "our injustice can beat up your injustice." It's simply an objective assessment of the scope of the abortion crisis: abortion is the priority pro-life issue because it's the most widespread assault on human dignity in history, taking the lives of more than 73 million children in the world each year.[3] An estimated 55.4 million people around the world die each year from all other causes *combined.*[4]

Abortion remains the leading cause of death in the United States,[5] taking more than 800,000 lives annually.[6]

Again, there's nothing wrong when somebody answers the call to invest themselves in addressing world hunger or capital punishment. But given the sheer scope of human carnage wrought by abortion, pro-lifers should be afforded the same opportunity to focus their efforts on ending abortion without having their motives questioned.

Point 2: The Character of Pro-lifers Should Have No Bearing on the Morality of Abortion

When abortion advocates can't effectively attack your arguments, they often attack *you*. Their goal is to discredit you—usually as they brand you a hypocrite to try to undermine your moral authority.

Of course, whether any individual pro-lifer fails to live out his or her pro-life convictions has no bearing on whether those pro-life convictions are true or false. If an animal-rights advocate were filmed kicking a dog, it wouldn't somehow make animal abuse *right*. In the same way, ad hominem attacks that point out pro-lifers' shortcomings don't justify the violence of abortion.

Even if we pro-lifers were a bunch of self-righteous hypocrites who hate women, want children to grow up in poverty, and think all immigrants should be executed at the border, we still don't have the right to kill a baby girl who has done nothing wrong in the womb.

Here are three of the most common accusations pro-lifers face—and how to respond to them.

1. *"Pro-lifers don't care about women in need. They care only about unborn children—and only until those children are born."* This claim sounds good in a debate, but there's no truth to it.

    Pregnancy help centers dramatically outnumber abortion centers 5 to 1. These centers provide or refer for material support, parent education, counseling, medical care, housing, and anything else a pregnant woman might need to get through her pregnancy *and beyond*—all at no charge. Many of the services provided continue years after the mother delivers her child, as the staff members and volunteers at pregnancy help centers establish long-lasting relationships with the women and families they serve.

Pregnancy help centers usually receive no government funding. That means that all the help provided to women and families in need is done through the generosity of pro-lifers who selflessly donate to establish and sustain pregnancy help centers around the world.

To find out more about the help available from a pregnancy center where you live, visit 40daysforlife.com/pregnancyhelp.

2. *"How many unwanted babies have you adopted?"* Pro-abortion passersby at 40 Days for Life vigils often ask this question, suggesting that a person cannot take a pro-life stand without offering to adopt the child scheduled to be aborted.

These hecklers don't realize (or perhaps don't care) that many 40 Days for Life volunteers have adopted or offered to adopt children who would otherwise be aborted. (And not just healthy babies. Countless pro-lifers are willing to welcome babies with special needs into their families.)

Certainly, it is courageous and laudable to offer to adopt children in need, but not every pro-lifer is in a position to adopt a child. That doesn't make abortion acceptable. After all, nobody would suggest that you can only oppose child abuse if you adopt every abused child. And nobody would suggest that you can only oppose the murder of an eleven-year-old child unless you try to adopt the eleven-year-old child.

Furthermore, many pro-lifers who aren't able to adopt do their part by supporting pregnancy help centers, which help birth mothers and fathers succeed at parenting *or* make adoption arrangements.

3. *"Why don't you feed the homeless or take care of kids who have already been born?"* The critique that we should serve people who have already been born suggests that passage through the birth canal is the source of human dignity. But unborn children—though small and hidden—are still unique human beings with their own distinct genetic code. There's simply no scientific, medical, philosophical, or religious basis for giving preference to human beings based on which side of the birth canal we find them on.

We don't discriminate against human beings at other stages of development. Imagine criticizing a breastfeeding mom for not caring about her children who can now eat table food or a dentist who doesn't care about children until after they cut teeth. It would be absurd!

If anything, the unique vulnerability of unborn children makes them *more* worthy of our attention. Lacking a voice to speak up in their own defense, unborn babies are marginalized more than any other demographic, which is why pro-lifers spend their time working and praying to end abortion.

Ultimately, pro-lifers look forward to the day abortion ends, so we can spend more time serving those who have been born. After all, nobody gets heckled serving in a soup kitchen.

Point 3: Anyone Can Oppose the Killing of Children

"Oh look, another old, white Republican male telling women what they can do with their bodies."

Identity politics is king these days, so it's not surprising when abortion supporters try to place you in a box. If they can categorize you as belonging to another tribe, you become the enemy, and it's easier for them to write off your values as irrelevant.

But the dignity of human life isn't a team sport. It's universal. You don't need to be a Christian (or white or male or a Republican) to oppose the killing of children.

The post-World War II Nuremburg Trials charged high-ranking Nazi officials with perpetrating crimes against humanity and genocide.[7] The defendants tried to avoid responsibility for their crimes by claiming they were "just following orders."[8]

The world swiftly rejected this excuse. Why? Because the International Military Tribunal was made up of self-righteous Christians trying to force their religion down the throat of the Nazis? Hardly.

"The charge of crimes against humanity emerged from a bigger idea: that all humans, no matter their nationality, race or religion, are entitled to certain basic rights to enable them to flourish and live with dignity," wrote Adam Wagner in *The Jewish Chronicle*. "The simple truth understood by the pioneers of the modern human rights movement was that a society founded on human rights principles could not also be genocidal."[9]

In other words, truths about the dignity of the human person are so obvious, so clear, and so universal that they transcend the boundaries of creed, culture, politics, and national borders.

By 1948, the Universal Declaration of Human Rights codified some of these truths, in part noting that

- Everyone has the right to life, liberty and security of person.
- No one shall be subjected to cruel, inhuman or degrading behavior.
- Everyone has the right to recognition as a person before the law.[10]

In short: human rights are for everyone, without exception. Why are the unborn excluded?

"You have no right to impose your religious beliefs on others!" abortion supporters shout at pro-lifers. But we don't need religion to tell us human life begins at fertilization; we only need to look at a biology textbook. That a new, unique, and unrepeatable human being comes into existence at the moment of conception is neither a religious statement nor an article of faith. It's empirical science.

So the question isn't "When does human life begin?" The question is "Is it ever acceptable to kill an innocent human being?"

And you don't have to be a Christian to oppose killing the innocent.

The notion that it's wrong to kill an innocent human is a universal principle of the natural moral law that spans religions, cultures, languages, and national borders. Christians, Jews, Muslims, people of other religions, and even atheists oppose abortion despite holding differing (or even a lack of) religious beliefs.

Striving to end abortion isn't the imposition of a religious belief; it's a recognition of the humanity of the pre-born child—and the rights endowed to all human beings.

Abortion shouldn't be a partisan issue either. But because politicians have taken it upon themselves to legalize, promote, and fund abortion, there is a common misconception that it is a merely political issue. This is a mistake with deadly ramifications.

No government has the authority to deny any individual person's right to life. Any law that says otherwise is an unjust law, and people of conscience are bound to reject and disobey it—regardless of their political affiliation.

From slavery to state-sponsored genocides, history is filled with horrific injustices. It's never partisan politics that motivates people to resist those injustices but a recognition of the dignity of all human beings. It's time for people of goodwill to set aside their partisan differences and unite in defense of abortion-vulnerable children.

What to Say When They Try to Change the Subject

1. Abortion is the preeminent human-rights issue because it's the most widespread and most direct attack on human beings.

2. Attacks on the character of pro-lifers are often dishonest and always a distraction. Even if they were true, they still wouldn't justify killing babies.

3. You don't need to be a Christian or a Republican (or a member of any other group) to respect the universality of human rights.

The Ultimate Argument

Hope has two beautiful daughters;
their names are Anger and Courage.
Anger at the way things are, and Courage
to see that they do not remain as they are.
— St. Augustine of Hippo

Being asked to speak at the Harvard commencement is quite an honor. But in 1982, Harvard had to settle for its third choice after being turned down by both a famous actor and Supreme Court Justice Sandra Day O'Connor. The Harvard commencement backup speaker powerfully addressed global issues and spoke eloquently about poverty and the role of America in the world.

And then, the speech took an unexpected turn when the speaker said, "It is something unbelievable that today a mother, herself, murders her own child, afraid of having to feed one more child, afraid to educate one more child. A nation, people, family that allows that, that accepts that, they are the poorest of the poor."

The Harvard commencement speaker that day was Mother Teresa.

Coverage in *John Harvard's Journal* noted, "Mother Teresa spoke with an almost mesmerizing conviction. . . . What she said struck many listeners as anomalous in Harvard Yard on

Class Day, but she received a long, standing ovation from the unusually large crowd come to hear a saintly woman."[1]

The world is desperately starving for something from *you*.

God wants it from you, and your family needs it from you. Those suffering from an abortion in their past and those having an abortion as you read this need something from you. The medical professionals who bring pain and hell upon themselves—and upon others—when they participate in abortion all need something from you.

They all need you to become a saint.

Jesus Christ died to make your sanctification possible. The strongest argument against abortion or any sin or injustice is sanctity. Many great Christians and saints who have gone before us admonished us to kill that which prevents us from becoming saints.

There is but one person on earth who can prevent you from being a saint: you. As many of the saints have said, "I know the problem, Lord, and the problem is me."

When we think and talk about saints, there is a temptation to distance ourselves from them. You might even be saying, "Come on, this is a pro-life apologetics book. Being a saint sounds good, but we need to win arguments, pass legislation, and end abortion."

We agree. The arguments in this book are designed and proven to do just that—and in many scenarios. But these arguments are not the strongest arguments against abortion. The strongest case we can make against abortion and in defense of life is the witness of our daily battle to live and struggle to become saints. And this struggle is not against "flesh and blood" but against our true enemy in this fight: the Devil.

We've never empowered a woman to choose life or helped an abortion worker to leave his job using superior arguments and logic. We've helped free them from the chains of abortion by helping them to understand they were made for heaven. As important as strong arguments are, nothing appeals to a person's heart more than our love. And we cannot truly love those who advocate for and participate in the barbaric murder of children unless we continuously draw closer to Jesus Christ.

Saints do not live on holy cards, statues, or museums. They live in the sweat, tears, and joy of witnessing the love of Jesus Christ to the world through their love of Him and neighbor. No one argues with a saint, and no saint needs vindication on Twitter.

Saints don't become obnoxious, self-righteous know-it-alls convinced that we are saints because we defend life and oppose abortion. Quite the opposite. Nor does it mean that we turn into lunatics and climb the flagpoles of abortion facilities to demand repentance from everyone in the parking lot. Our own track record shows that we don't endorse this approach and would not tolerate it.

Instead, our call to sainthood means that we always recognize our own sins and our culpability for our words and actions because one day, we will answer for what we have done and said—and what we have failed to do and say. Our strongest weapon for fighting and ending abortion is prayer, which draws us closer to Him who conquered death on the cross.

The Harvard student body didn't give Mother Teresa a standing ovation that day because they agreed with everything she said or because she was a sweet nun or because they didn't want to be rude. Much of what she said could be interpreted as rude or offensive. They stood because the love of Jesus Christ radiated from her. It was irresistible.

You should have great confidence in using the material in this book to win arguments and convert abortion supporters. But you can't cut this last chapter and expect to go out and conquer the world without striving for sanctity. That's because the most powerful arrow in your quiver is the resolve to become a saint. Saints don't merely win arguments or convert a few minds to their view; they change and heal the world.

The culture of death is a battlefield. Even as the war rages on, countless casualties—those wounded physically, emotionally, mentally, and spiritually by abortion—need healing. At the same time, we plant seeds to prevent future bloodshed. Our sanctification is needed in a world starving for truth and love. God gives each of us the grace to grow closer to Him and sanctify our lives—body and soul—no matter who we are or where we are from.

When the 2008 Planned Parenthood Employee of the Year, Abby Johnson, witnessed an abortion for the first time, she witnessed the brutal murder of a thirteen-week-old baby. She came right to our office, which at the time was located next door to Planned Parenthood. Her conversion is well documented in her beautiful book and major motion picture, *Unplanned*.

As our friendship grew in the days and weeks that followed her conversion, we rarely discussed abortion or the fact that, at the time, she still favored allowing some abortions. In all that time, she only asked one pointed question: "What is that?"

She pointed to a painting hanging in our office, which she had noticed several times and finally asked about.

"Good question. That's you."

The image was a copy of Rembrandt's famous painting *The Return of the Prodigal Son*.

With Abby—as with many other former abortion workers we have helped—we sometimes feel a need to thoroughly convince them that abortion is something they never want to be part of again, lest they fall into temptation and go back to Planned Parenthood. But Abby's story always reminds us what abortion workers and advocates are seeking. They seek love; they seek Jesus Christ.

They, like us, are not Home. We are pilgrims, not permanent residents of this world, a world that tells parents it's responsible to kill their own children. Abortion is a crisis of love, and there is no better way to be a channel of love than living our lives as an instrument of the Author of Life.

Acknowledgments

Thank you to the 40 Days for Life board of directors for their enthusiasm and support to get this book out during such a busy time for our mission. Special thanks to Matt Britton, our general counsel.

What would we do without our wonderful copyeditor Lisa Parnell? Every time we work with you, we hope we have another book in us—you are a pleasure and a joy! We are grateful to Jeanette Gillespie for designing the book cover.

Thank you to the folks at Daily Wire and Matt Walsh for writing the foreword and believing in this project during such a critical time for our nation.

Thank you to the entire 40 Days for Life team who makes this work possible and the local campaign leaders who are our inspiration to do this work every day.

Finally, to our wonderful wives. Writing any book, but especially one like this, is time consuming and takes much sacrifice on top of our other work responsibilities. Thank you for your support, feedback, and love. You always seem to know what to say when we need it to keep us on track.

Endnotes

Introduction

1. "Unintended Pregnancy and Abortion Worldwide," Guttmacher Institute, July 2020, https://www.guttmacher.org/fact-sheet/induced -abortion-worldwide#.

Chapter 1

1. Judith Jarvis Thomson, "A Defense of Abortion," *Philosophy & Public Affairs* 1:1 (Fall 1971), 47–66, https://spot.colorado.edu/ ~heathwoo/Phil160,Fall02/thomson.htm.

Chapter 2

1. Alia E. Dastagir, "Rape and incest account for hardly any abortions. So why are they now a focus?" *USA Today*, May 24, 2019, https://www .usatoday.com/story/news/nation/2019/05/24/rape-and-incest-account- few-abortions-so-why-all-attention/1211175001/.

Chapter 3

1. Peter Kreeft, "The Kalam Argument," https://www.peterkreeft. com/topics-more/20_arguments-gods-existence.htm.

2. "Pope John Paul II Opening Address at the Puebla Conference," delivered January 28, 1979 https://www.catholicculture.org/culture/ library/view.cfm?recnum=5529.

3. Katie McCann, "The Miracle of Human Development: Life Begins Long Before She's Born," October 24, 2013, https://www.lifenews. com/2013/10/24/the-miracle-of-human-development-life-begins -long-before-shes-born/.

4. Roe v. Wade, 410 U.S. 113 (1973), https://supreme.justia.com/ cases/federal/us/410/113/.

5. Tony Magliano, "How marvelous is the miracle of life," May 19, 2016, *Catholic Herald*, http://www.madisoncatholicherald.org/making adifference/6393-how-marvelous-is-the-miracle-of-life.html.

6. "Cloning Human Beings, Report and Recommendations of the National Bioethics Advisory Commission" (Rockville, MD: GPO, 1997), glossary, 2.

7. Sarah Terzo, "Science is clear: Each new human life beings at fertilization," January 13, 2013, https://www.liveaction.org/news/life -begins-at-conception-science-teaches/.

8. Steven Jacobs, "Biologists' Consensus on 'When Life Begins,'" July 25, 2018, SSRN, https://ssrn.com/abstract=3211703 or http://dx.doi. org/10.2139/ssrn.3211703.

9. Peter Kreeft, "Human Personhood Begins at Conception," http:// www.peterkreeft.com/topics-more/personhood.htm.

10. Scott Klusendorf, "Five Bad Ways to Argue About Abortion," *Pro-Life 101: a User Friendly Guide to Making Your Case on Campus* (1997), https://www.issuesetcarchive.org/issues_site/resource/archives/ klsdorf1.htm.

Chapter 4

1. Kelsey Bolar, "New Study: 'Sex Selection Abortions Is a Global Problem,' Including in US," April 12, 2016, https://www.dailysignal .com/2016/04/12/new-study-sex-selection-abortion-is-a-global-problem -including-in-us/.

2. Shawn Carney, *40 Days for Life* (Nashville: Cappella Books, 2013), 230.

Chapter 5

1. Miley Cyrus (@mileycyrus), Instagram photo, June 4, 2019, https://www.instagram.com/p/ByStizPJcO6/

2. Oliver Herzfeld, "Was Miley Cyrus' 'Abortion Is Healthcare' Cake A Rip-Off?" June 11, 2019, https://www.forbes.com/sites/oliver herzfeld/2019/06/11/was-miley-cyrus-abortion-is-healthcare-cake-a-rip- off/?sh=3034edd76909.

3. "How often is abortion necessary to 'save the life of the mother'?" October 19, 2012, https://www.nrlc.org/archive/abortion/pba/HowOften AbortionNecessarySaveMother.pdf on May 8, 2020.

4. "Abortion," https://news.gallup.com/poll/1576/abortion.aspx.

5. Ibid.

6. "Abortion Refusal Laws," NARAL, https://www.prochoiceamerica.org/issue/abortion-refusal-laws/.

7. Jane Clark, "'Pro-Choice,' Ha—The ACLU Went after Catholic Hospitals for Choosing against Abortion," April 14, 2016, http://www.nationalreview.com/article/434045/aclu-abortion-catholic-hospitals-choose-be-pro-life-despite-its-lawsuit.

8. Staff, "Reasons U.S. Women Have Abortions: Quantitative and Qualitative Perspectives," *Perspectives on Sexual and Reproductive Health* 37:3 (September 2005), 110–18, https://www.guttmacher.org/journals/psrh/2005/reasons-us-women-have-abortions-quantitative-and-qualitative-perspectives.

9. Luu Ireland, MD, "Who are the 1 in 4 American women who choose abortion?" May 30, 2019, University of Massachusetts Medical School News, https://www.umassmed.edu/news/news-archives/2019/05/who-are-the-1-in-4-american-women-who-choose-abortion/.

10. Sarah Terzo, "Former abortionist: Abortion is never medically necessary to save the life of a mother," October 21, 2016, https://www.liveaction.org/news/former-abortionist-abortion-is-never-medically-necessary-to-save-the-life-of-the-mother/.

11. Staff, "'Pro-choice' co-founder rips abortion industry," World Net Daily, December 20, 2002, http://www.wnd.com/2002/12/16344/.

12. Holly Yan, "Nurses, other non-physicians can perform abortions in California," October 10, 2013, https://www.cnn.com/2013/10/10/politics/california-nurse-practitioners-abortions/index.html.

13. Regina Barton, "Maine governor signs bill allowing nonphysicians to perform abortions," June 11, 2019, https://www.washingtonexaminer.com/news/maine-governor-signs-bill-allowing-nonphysicians-to-perform-abortions.

14. Caroline Kelly, "Virginia governor signs abortion protections into law," April 10, 2020, https://www.cnn.com/2020/04/10/politics/virginia-abortion-protections/index.html.

15. Elizabeth Shadigian, MD, "Reviewing the Medical Evidence: Short and Long-Term Physical Consequences of Induced Abortion," testimony before the South Dakota Task Force to Study Abortion, September 21, 2005; Americans United for Life, https://aul.org/2013/08/13/known-health-risks-of-abortion/.

16. "Authorities: Woman died from abortion complications," February 21, 2013, https://www.usatoday.com/story/news/nation/2013/02/21/woman-late-term-abortion-death/1935799/.

17. Alexis Shaw, "Chicago Woman's Family Lawyers Up After Abortion-Related Death," July 24, 2012, https://abcnews.go.com/US/chicago-womans-family-lawyers-abortion-related-death/story?id=16845276.

18. Mary Kilpatrick, "Woman died of complications during an abortion, Cuyahoga County Medical Examiner rules," May 30, 2014, https://www.cleveland.com/metro/2014/05/woman_died_of_compli cations_du.html.

19. Cassy Fiano-Chesser, "New study confirms higher risk of mental health disorders after abortion," August 26, 2016, https://www.liveaction.org/news/new-study-confirms-higher-risk-of-mental-health-disorders-after-abortion/.

20. Priscilla K. Coleman, "Abortion and mental health: quantitative synthesis and analysis of research published 1995–2009," January 2, 2018, http://bjp.rcpsych.org/content/199/3/180.

21. Planned Parenthood of New York City, September 18, 2001, http://web.archive.org/web/20011112105430/http://www.ppnyc.org/new/releases/wtcservices.html.

22. Staff, "Katrina Evacuees Qualify for Free Birth Control and Other Reproductive Health Care Services," September 22, 2005, https://www.plannedparenthood.org/about-us/newsroom/press-releases/katrina.

23. Brittany Shammas, "After Irma and Maria, Planned Parenthood Offers Free Emergency Services in Florida," November 27, 2017, https://www.miaminewtimes.com/news/planned-parenthood-offers-free-emergency-services-in-florida-after-irma-maria-9852849.

24. Carole Joffe, "When Hurricane Harvey Hit, Texas Abortion Providers Stepped Up," September 12, 2017, https://rewire.news/article/2017/09/12/hurricane-harvey-texas-abortion-providers-stepped/.

25. "Pro-life group rebukes Planned Parenthood for sending birth control to Haiti," January 21, 2010, https://www.catholicnewsagency.com/news/pro-life_group_rebukes_planned_parenthood_for_sending_birth_control_to_haiti.

26. "Resilience and commitment in the aftermath of Mexico's devastating earthquakes," n.d., https://www.ippf.org/resource/resilience-and-commitment-aftermath-mexicos-devastating-earthquakes.

27. "Emergency appeal for the earthquake and tsunami in Indonesia," October 2, 2018, https://www.ippf.org/blogs/emergency-appeal-earthquake-and-tsunami-indonesia.

28. Beth LeBlanc, "Anti-abortion groups criticize Whitmer's quip that abortion 'life-sustaining,'" April 20, 2020, https://www.detroit news.com/story/news/politics/2020/04/20/gov-whitmer-comment -abortion-life-sustaining/5166518002/.

29. Susan Berry, MD, "Planned Parenthood seeks donations of protective medical equipment for abortions during pandemic," April 1, 2020, https://www.breitbart.com/politics/2020/04/01/planned-parent hood-seeks-donations-of-protective-medical-equipment-for-abortions- during-pandemic/.

Chapter 7

1. Kristin Romey, "Ancient Mass Child Sacrifice May Be World's Largest," April 26, 2018, https://www.nationalgeographic.com/news/ 2018/04/mass-child-human-animal-sacrifice-peru-chimu-science/.

2. Ibid.

3. Sam Jones, "Peru: skeletons of 227 victims unearthed at world's largest child sacrifice site," August 29, 2019, https://www.theguardian. com/world/2019/aug/29/peru-huanchaco-sacrificial-site-skeletons.

4. Romey, "Ancient Mass Child Sacrifice May Be World's Largest."

5. "Combating climate change with . . . abortion?" September 23, 2019, *40 Days for Life Podcast*, 4:39, https://www.40daysforlife.com/ combating-climate-change-withabortionpodcast-season-4-episode-39.

6. Thomas Malthus, "An Essay on the Principle of Population" (1798), http://www.esp.org/books/malthus/population/malthus.pdf.

7. German Lopez, "How the world went from 170 million people to 7.3 billion, in one map," January 30, 2016, https://www.vox. com/2016/1/30/10872878/world-population-map.

8. "Natural Family Planning: The Best Worst Thing Ever," October 18, 2014, Population Research Institute, https://youtu.be/OXrN9HhnCcM.

9. Ibid.

10. "Combating climate change with . . . abortion?" *40 Days for Life Podcast.*

11. Andre Tartar, Hannah Recht, and Yue Qiu, "The Global Fertility Crash," October 30, 2019, https://www.bloomberg.com/graphics/2019 -global-fertility-crash/.

12. Megan Molteni, "The World Might Actually Run Out of People," February 4, 2019, https://www.wired.com/story/the-world-might-actually -run-out-of-people/.

13. "Urbanization: Who's Afraid of the Big Bad City," Population Research Institute, June 7, 2013, https://youtu.be/7QWAXWhtSCQ.

14. "Food: There's Lots of It," Population Research Institute, May 3, 2010, https://youtu.be/OXrN9HhnCcM.

15. "2019 U.S. Population Estimates Continue to Show the Nation's Growth Is Slowing," release CB19-198, December 30, 2019, US Census Bureau, https://www.census.gov/newsroom/press-releases/2019/popest-nation.html.

16. Perry Lindstrom, "U.S. energy-related carbon dioxide fell by 2.8% in 2019, slightly below 2017 levels," U.S. Energy Information Administration, May 5, 2020, https://www.eia.gov/todayinenergy/detail.php?id=43615.

17. Ahmad O. Al-Khowaiter, "Saudi Aramco exec: Capturing carbon emissions can help combat climate change," June 10, 2020, CNN Business Perspectives, https://www.cnn.com/2020/06/10/perspectives/carbon-capture-saudi-aramco/index.html.

18. Jeff McMahon, "Coal Is Collapsing Faster Than Ever, Leaving U.S. Power Cleaner," May 11, 2020, https://www.forbes.com/sites/jeffmcmahon/2020/05/11/carbon-intensity-of-us-power-plunges-as-coal-collapses-faster/?sh=4f8ca65c264c.

19. Grace Melton, "Pro-Life Nations Reject U.N.'s Cultural Colonialism on Abortion, Population Control," the Heritage Foundation, November 20, 2019, https://www.heritage.org/life/commentary/pro-life-nations-reject-uns-cultural-colonialism-abortion-population-control.

20. "West imposing abortion on Africa is attempt at cultural supremacy," the Christian Institute, July 20, 2017, https://www.christian.org.uk/news/west-imposing-abortion-africa-attempt-cultural-supremacy/.

21. "Abortion in Africa," Guttmacher Institute, March 2018, https://www.guttmacher.org/sites/default/files/factsheet/ib_aww-africa.pdf.

22. Steven Mosher, "Obama wants more contraceptives for Nigeria. Nigerians want none of it," August 11, 2014, https://www.lifesitenews.com/opinion/obama-wants-more-contraceptives-for-nigeria.-nigerians-want-none-of-it.

23. "Aborting Africa," August 22, 2017, *40 Days for Life Podcast*, episode 85, https://www.40daysforlife.com/en/2017/08/22/podcast-85.

24. Diane Montagna, "US Won't Help Fight Boko Haram Until Nigeria Accepts Homosexuality, Birth Control, Bishop Says," February 17, 2015, https://aleteia.org/2015/02/17/us-wont-help-fight-boko-haram-until-nigeria-accepts-homosexuality-birth-control-bishop-says/3/.

25. Jonathan Abbamonte, "Kenyans, Pro-Life Advocates Resist Promotion of Abortion & Sex Education at U.N. Nairobi Conference," Population Research Institute, December 3, 2019, https://www.pop.org/kenyans-pro-life-advocates-resist-promotion-of-abortion-sex-education-at-u-n-nairobi-conference/.

26. Sophia Feingold, "Pro-Life in Africa: 'What We Hold in Common Is This Value for Family,'" *National Catholic Register*, April 27, 2016, https://www.ncregister.com/daily-news/pro-life-in-africa-what-we-hold-in-common-is-this-value-for-family.

27. Staff, "In Ecuador, pro-life groups protest U.N. abortion conditions on coronavirus aid," May 17, 2020, https://www.catholicnewsagency.com/news/in-ecuador-pro-life-groups-protest-un-abortion-conditions-on-coronavirus-aid-22027

28. Stefano Gennarini, "The Future of the Pro-Life Movement Is in Africa," *Public Discourse*, April 12, 2018, https://www.thepublicdiscourse.com/2018/04/21339/.

29. "It Takes A Village: A Shared Agenda for Social and Behavior Change in Family Planning," August 2019, https://breakthroughaction andresearch.org/wp-content/uploads/2019/08/It-Takes-A-Village-Shared-Agenda-SBC-FP-2019AUG12.pdf.

30. "Continent and Region Populations 2021," https://world populationreview.com/continents/

31. Hannah Ritchie and Max Roser, "CO_2 and Greenhouse Gas Emissions," August 2020, https://ourworldindata.org/co2-and-other -greenhouse-gas-emissions#annual-co2-emissions.

32. Ibid.

33. Wesley J. Smith, "The return of nature worship," Acton Institute, August 6, 2018, https://www.acton.org/religion-liberty/volume -28-number-3/return-nature-worship.

34. Catherine Clifford, "Elon Musk and Jack Ma agree: The biggest problem the world will face is population collapse," August 30, 2019, https://www.cnbc.com/2019/08/30/elon-musk-jack-ma-biggest-problem-world-will-face-is-population-drop.html.

Chapter 8

1. Thomas W. Jacobsen and Wm. Robert Johnston, *Abortion Worldwide Report* (GLC Publications, LLC, 2018).

2. Ibid.

3. Rachel K. Jones, Elizabeth Witwer, and Jenna Jerman, "Abortion Incidence and Service Availability in the United States, 2017," Guttmacher Institute, September 2019, https://www.guttmacher.org/report/abortion-incidence-service-availability-us-2017.

4. Nicole Stacy, "Pro-life Pregnancy Centers Served 2 Million People, Saved Communities $161M in 2017," Charlotte Lozier Institute, September 5, 2018, https://lozierinstitute.org/pro-life-pregnancy-centers-served-2-million-people-saved-communities-161m-in-2017/.

5. "Contraceptive Access Lags," January 30, 2014, https://www.plannedparenthood.org/about-us/newsroom/press-releases/contraceptive-access-lags.

6. "Setting the Record Straight on Contraceptives," Center for Reproductive Rights," September 2009, https://reproductiverights.org/sites/default/files/documents/pub_fac_slovak_contramyths_9.08_WEB.pdf.

7. "Promoting Access to Contraception and Opposing Threats to Its Availability at Home and Abroad," American Civil Liberties Union, https://www.aclu.org/other/promoting-access-contraception-and-opposing-threats-its-availability-home-and-abroad.

8. Frances Kissling, "Should Abortion Be Prevented?" *Conscience* magazine, Winter 2006–7, https:/www.catholicsforchoice.org/issues_publications/should-abortion-be-prevented/.

9. "Birth Control," NARAL Pro-Choice Connecticut, https://www.prochoicect.org/issue/birth-control/.

10. Jim Kessler, Lanae Erickson, Sarah Trumble, "Abortion: Reducing the Need, Protecting the Right," October 1, 2012, https://www.thirdway.org/report/abortion-reducing-the-need-protecting-the-right.

11. Ibid.

12. Ibid.

13. Susan M. Shaw, "Can Christians come together to reduce the need for abortion?" Baptist News Global, February 15, 2019, https://baptistnews.com/article/can-christians-come-together-to-reduce-the-need-for-abortion/#.YKuzpi9h2X0.

14. Robert A. Hatcher and Deborah Kowal, "Birth Control," National Center for Biotechnology Information, https://www.ncbi.nlm.nih.gov/books/NBK283/.

15. Donna Harrison, "Contraception That Kills," July 8, 2014, https://www.nationalreview.com/2014/07/contraception-kills-donna-harrison/.

16. Randy Alcorn, "Does the birth control pill cause abortions?" Eternal Perspective Ministries, 2011, https://www.epm.org/static/uploads/downloads/bcpill.pdf.

17. "Antiabortion Activists In Their Own Words: Contraception Is Abortion," Guttmacher Institute, July 24, 2008, https://www.guttmacher.org/antiabortion-activists-their-own-words-contraception-abortion.

18. Dianne N. Irving, testimony, New Jersey State Senate Committee, November 4, 2002, University Faculty for Life, http://www.uffl.org/irving/irvnewjersey.htm.

19. Rachel K. Jones, "Reported contraceptive use in the month of becoming pregnant among U.S. abortion patients in 2000 and 2014," *Contraception* 97 (2018): 309–12, https://www.contraceptionjournal.org/action/showPdf?pii=S0010-7824%2818%2930003-9.

20. Ibid.

21. "About Half of U.S. Abortion Patients Report Using Contraception in the Month They Became Pregnant," Guttmacher Institute, January 11, 2018, https://www.guttmacher.org/news-release/2018/about-half-us-abortion-patients-report-using-contraception-month-they-became.

22. Jones, "Reported contraceptive use in the month of becoming pregnant among U.S. abortion patients in 2000 and 2014."

23. "Over half of UK women who sought abortion last year used contraceptives," Catholic News Agency, August 4, 2017, https://angelusnews.com/local/la-catholics/over-half-of-uk-women-who-sought-abortion-last-year-used-contraceptives/.

24. William Crawley, "The pope was right about condoms, says Harvard HIV expert," *Will & Testament* (blog), March 29, 2009, https://www.bbc.co.uk/blogs/ni/2009/03/aids_expert_who_defended_the_p.html.

25. Ibid.

26. "Over half of UK women who sought abortion last year used contraceptives."

27. Planned Parenthood of Southeastern Pa. v. Casey, 505 U.S. 833 (1992), Justia Opinion Summary and Annotations, https://supreme.justia.com/cases/federal/us/505/833/.

28. Jones, "Reported contraceptive use in the month of becoming pregnant among U.S. abortion patients in 2000 and 2014."

29. "Data Brief 229: Mortality in the United States, 2014," Centers for Disease Control and Prevention, https://www.cdc.gov/nchs/data/databriefs/db229_table.pdf#1.

30. Jones, "Reported contraceptive use in the month of becoming pregnant among U.S. abortion patients in 2000 and 2014."

31. "Data Brief 229: Mortality in the United States, 2014."

Chapter 9

1. *All in the Family*, CBS.

2. Lisa Lerer, "When Joe Biden Voted to Let States Overturn Roe v. Wade," March 29, 2019, https://www.nytimes.com/2019/03/29/us/politics/biden-abortion-rights.html.

3. Caitlin Flanagan, "Losing the *Rare* in 'Safe, Legal, and Rare,'" December 6, 2019, https://www.theatlantic.com/ideas/archive/2019/12/the-brilliance-of-safe-legal-and-rare/603151/.

4. "Gore Lying about Stance on Abortion; . . . What Changed His Mind?" *Greensboro News & Record*, January 24, 2015, https://greensboro.com/gore-lying-about-stance-on-abortion-al-gore-once-wrote/article_9b54dbca-4972-52ee-9ca8-1f5745cc38f4.html.

5. "Pro-birth isn't synonymous with pro-life," February 22, 2018, https://www.thetelegraph.com/news/article/Pro-birth-isn-t-synonymous-with-pro-life-12646226.php.

6. Christopher Blosser, "Two Letters," *First Things* (blog), August 30, 2009, https://www.firstthings.com/blogs/firstthoughts/2009/08/two-letters.

7. Sue Halpern, "How Republicans Became Anti-Choice," November 8, 2018, *New York Review*, https://www.nybooks.com/articles/2018/11/08/how-republicans-became-anti-choice/.

8. John Murdock, "The Future of the Pro-Life Democrat," *National Affairs* 47 (Winter 2020), https://nationalaffairs.com/publications/detail/the-future-of-the-pro-life-democrat.

9. Steven Ertelt, "Jimmy Carter: Democrats Should Abandon Pro-Abortion Position," March 29, 2012, https://www.lifenews.com/2012/03/29/jimmy-carter-democrats-should-abandon-pro-abortion-position/.

10. Anna North, "How abortion became a partisan issue in America," April 10, 2019, https://www.vox.com/2019/4/10/18295513/abortion-2020-roe-joe-biden-democrats-republicans.

11. Halpern, "How Republicans Became Anti-Choice."

12. Daniel K. Williams, "The GOP's Abortion Strategy: Why Pro-Choice Republicans Became Pro-Life in the 1970s," *Journal of Policy History* 23:4, October 25, 2011, https://www.cambridge.org/core/journals/journal-of-policy-history/article/gops-abortion-strategy-why-prochoice-republicans-became-prolife-in-the-1970s/C7EC0E0C0F5FF1F4488AA47C787DEC01.

13. Halpern, "How Republicans Became Anti-Choice."

14. "Republicans' History on Abortion," editorial, *National Catholic Register*, September 5, 2020, https://www.ncregister.com/commentaries/republicans-history-on-abortion.

15. Eric C. Miller, "When Being Pro-Life Did Not Mean Being Conservative," May 31, 2016, https://religionandpolitics.org/2016/05/31/when-being-pro-life-did-not-mean-being-conservative/.

16. Adam Wren, "'It Was Riotous': An Oral History of the GOP's Last Open Convention," April 5, 2016, https://www.politico.com/magazine/story/2016/04/1976-convention-oral-history-213793.

17. Halpern, "How Republicans Became Anti-Choice."

18. Miller, "When Being Pro-Life Did Not Mean Being Conservative."

19. Ryan P. Burge, "Which Party Has Become More Polarized on Abortion?" *Religion in Public* (blog), June 10, 2019, https://religioninpublic.blog/2019/06/10/which-party-has-become-more-polarized-on-abortion/.

20. Gerhard Peters and John T. Woolley, "1976 Democratic Party Platform," the American Presidency Project, July 12, 1976, https://www.presidency.ucsb.edu/documents/1976-democratic-party-platform.

21. George McKenna, "Criss-Cross: Democrats, Republicans, and Abortion," *Human Life Review* (Summer/Fall 2006), https://humanlifereview.com/criss-cross-democrats-republicans-and-abortion-2/.

22. Ibid.

23. Murdock, "The Future of the Pro-Life Democrat."

24. Paul Kengor and Patricia Clark Doerner, "Reagan's Darkest Hour," January 22, 2008, https://www.nationalreview.com/2008/01/reagans-darkest-hour-paul-kengor-patricia-clark-doerner/.

25. Janet Hook, "On abortion, many have flip-flopped," March 11, 2007, https://www.latimes.com/archives/la-xpm-2007-mar-11-na-abortion11-story.html.

26. Kengor and Doerner, "Reagan's Darkest Hour."

27. Ibid.

28. Peters and Woolley, "Republican Party Platform of 1976," August 18, 1976, https://www.presidency.ucsb.edu/documents/republican-party-platform-1976.

29. "Republicans' History on Abortion."

30. Peters and Woolley, "1980 Democratic Party Platform, August 11, 1980, https://www.presidency.ucsb.edu/documents/1980-democratic-party-platform.

31. "Criss-Cross: Democrats, Republicans, and Abortion."

32. Peter Steinfels, "On abortion, as a former Pennsylvania governor showed, the silencing of opposing views continues in both political parties," June 3, 2000, https://www.nytimes.com/2000/06/03/us/beliefs-abortion-former-pennsylvania-governor-showed-silencing-opposing-views.html.

33. Peters and Woolley, "1992 Democratic Party Platform," July 13, 1992, https://www.presidency.ucsb.edu/documents/1992-democratic-party-platform.

34. Fred Barnes, "They'd Rather Switch Than Fight," March 5, 2007, https://www.washingtonexaminer.com/weekly-standard/theyd-rather-switch-than-fight.

35. Flanagan, "Losing the *Rare* in 'Safe, Legal, and Rare.'"

36. Ibid.

37. Wm. Robert Johnston, "Historical abortion statistics, United States," January 14, 2020, http://www.johnstonsarchive.net/policy/abortion/ab-unitedstates.html.

38. "Bishops' letter to President Clinton condemning Partial Birth Abortion Veto," April 16, 1996, https://www.catholicnewsagency.com/resources/abortion/partial-birth-abortion/bishops-letter-to-president-clinton-condemning-partial-birth-abortion-veto.

39. James O'Toole, "Silenced in '92, late Gov. Casey to get center stage," August 15, 2000, http://old.post-gazette.com/headlines/20000815caseysdemcon1.asp.

40. Steinfels, "On abortion, as a former Pennsylvania governor showed, the silencing of opposing views continues in both political parties."

41. Ibid.

42. Tim Reeves, Pete Leffler, Tom Lowry, "Casey Soundly Defeats Hafer; Landslide Returns Democrat to Governor's Mansion," November 7, 1990, https://www.mcall.com/news/mc-xpm-1990-11-07-2772199-story.html.

43. Steinfels, "On abortion, as a former Pennsylvania governor showed, the silencing of opposing views continues in both political parties."

44. Flanagan, "Losing the *Rare* in 'Safe, Legal, and Rare.'"

45. Anna North, "How the abortion debate moved away from 'safe, legal, and rare,'" October 18, 2019, https://www.vox.com/2019/10/18/20917406/abortion-safe-legal-and-rare-tulsi-gabbard.

46. Ibid.

47. Kathryn Jean Lopez, "*Slate* Warns of the FOCA Threat to Religious Liberty and Health Care in America," November 25, 2008, https://www.nationalreview.com/corner/slate-warns-foca-threat-religious-liberty-and-health-care-america-kathryn-jean-lopez/.

48. North, "How the abortion debate moved away from 'safe, legal, and rare.'"

49. Ibid.

50. Ibid.

51. Kristen Day and Charles Camosy, "Op-Ed: How the Democratic platform betrays millions of the party faithful," July 25, 2016, https://www.latimes.com/opinion/op-ed/la-oe-day-and-camosy-democratic-platform-abortion-20160725-snap-story.html.

52. Ibid.

53. "2020 Democratic Party Platform," August 2020, https://democrats.org/wp-content/uploads/sites/2/2020/08/2020-Democratic-Party-Platform.pdf.

54. John Fund, "The Extinction of Pro-Life Democrats in Congress," January 29, 2015, https://www.nationalreview.com/corner/extinction-pro-life-democrats-congress-john-fund/.

55. Myriam Renaud, "Hillary Clinton's Moral Conflicts on Abortion," August 6, 2016, https://www.theatlantic.com/politics/archive/2016/08/hillary-clinton-abortion/494723/.

Chapter 10

1. "The Note," *Seinfeld*, 3:1, September 18, 1991, https://www.imdb.com/title/tt0697741/characters/nm0000632.

2. Sarah Terzo, "5 quotes that show pro-abortion leaders know exactly what abortion is," July 16, 2015, https://www.lifesitenews.com/pulse/5-quotes-that-show-pro-abortion-leaders-know-exactly-what-abortion-is.

3. Lisa H Harris, "Second Trimester Abortion Provision: Breaking the Silence and Changing the Discourse," *Reproductive Health Matters* 16 (September 2, 2008), 74–81, https://doi.org/10.1016/S0968-8080(08)31396-2.

4. Judith Fetrow, "Don't Panic: The Sidewalk Counselor's Guidebook," Eternal Word Television Network, https://www.ewtn.com/catholicism/library/dont-panic-the-sidewalk-counselors-guidebook-12174.

5. Dr. Susan Berry, "Late-Term Abortionist: 'The Baby Has No Input in This As Far As I'm Concerned," August 27, 2019, https://www.breitbart.com/politics/2019/08/27/late-term-abortionist-the-baby-has-no-input-in-this-as-far-as-im-concerned/.

6. Joanna Brien and Ida Fairbairn, *Pregnancy and Abortion Counseling* (London: Routledge, 1996), 168.

7. Bruce Steir, *Jailhouse Journal of an OB/GYN* (Bloomington, IN: Author House, 2008), 81.

8. Sarah Terzo, "Abortionist gets honest: 'Yes, we end lives here . . . and I'm okay with that,'" April 8, 2019, https://www.liveaction.org/news/abortionists-end-lives-okay-that/.

9. Merle Hoffman, "Abortion–The 'Issue,'" *On the Issues* 12 (1989), https://www.ontheissuesmagazine.com/1989vol12/vol12_1989_1.php.

10. Sarah Terzo, "Abortionists agree: abortion is killing," March 15, 2013, https://www.liveaction.org/news/abortionists-agree-abortion-is-killing/.

11. Ibid.

12. Ibid.

13. Ibid.

14. Ibid.

15. Ibid.

16. Ibid.

17. Melanie Arter, "Carhart: Aborting Late-Term Baby 'Like Putting Meat in a Crock-Pot,'" June 14, 2013, https://www.cnsnews.com/news/article/carhart-aborting-late-term-baby-putting-meat-crock-pot.

Chapter 11

1. Cynthia Murdock, MD, "IVF Attrition Rate: Why Don't All Eggs Create Embryos?" Reproductive Medicine Associates of Connecticut, April 23, 2020, https://www.rmact.com/fertility-blog/ivf-attrition-rate.

2. Ibid.

3. Bassem Refaat, Elizabeth Dalton, William L. Ledger, "Ectopic pregnancy secondary to in vitro fertilisation-embryo transfer: pathogenic mechanisms and management strategies," April 12, 2015, https://www.ncbi.nlm.nih.gov/pmc/articles/PMC4403912/.

4. Kelly Burch, "12 IVF Truths No One Tells You About," *Healthy Way*, CCRM Fertility, https://www.ccrmivf.com/news-events/ivf-truths/.

5. Jennifer Lahl, "The Untold Harms of Surrogacy," July 13, 2020, https://www.nationalreview.com/2020/07/surrogacy-celebrity-baby-market-puts-women-at-risk/.

6. Jennifer Gerson Uffalussy, "The Cost of IVF: 4 Things I Learned While Battling Infertility," February 6, 2014, https://www.forbes.com/sites/learnvest/2014/02/06/the-cost-of-ivf-4-things-i-learned-while-battling-infertility/?sh=6c0c71b724dd.

7. Mary Pflum, "Nation's fertility clinics struggle with a growing number of abandoned embryos," August 12, 2019, https://www.nbcnews.com/health/features/nation-s-fertility-clinics-struggle-growing-number-abandoned-embryos-n1040806.

8. Rachel Gurevich, RN, "Options for What to Do With Extra Frozen Embryos After IVF," February 19, 2021, https://www.verywellfamily.com/extra-embryos-after-ivf-what-are-your-options-1960215.

9. Pflum, "Nation's fertility clinics struggle with a growing number of abandoned embryos."

10. The Associated Press, "Tens of thousands of embryos are stuck in limbo in fertility clinics," January 17, 2019, https://www.cbsnews.com/news/embryos-are-stuck-in-limbo-in-fertility-clinics/.

11. "The 50 largest cities in the United States," U.S. Census Bureau, the Poynter Institute, https://www.politifact.com/largestcities/.

12. "How Many Embryos Should You Transfer?" Keck School of Medicine of USC, https://uscfertility.org/fertility-treatments/many-embryos-transfer/.

13. Ibid.

14. "Surrogates and Abortion: What to Know Before Taking This Journey," https://surrogate.com/surrogates/pregnancy-and-health/surrogates-and-abortion-what-to-know-before-taking-this-journey/.

15. Carl Campanile, "Surrogate carrying triplets sues to stop forced abortion," January 4, 2016, https://nypost.com/2016/01/04/surrogate-mom-carrying-triplets-sues-to-stop-forced-abortion/.

16. Elizabeth Cohen, "Surrogate offered "$10,000 to abort baby," March 6, 2013, https://www.cnn.com/2013/03/04/health/surrogacy-kelley-legal-battle/index.html.

17. "Fertility Market Overview," May 2015, https://www.harris williams.com/sites/default/files/content/fertility_industry_overview_-_2015.05.19_v10.pdf.

18. "Sofia Vergara: US actress faces lawsuit 'from own embryos,'" December 8, 2016, https://www.bbc.com/news/world-us-canada-3825 2457.

19. Sarah E. Fendrick and Donald L. Zuhn Jr., "Patentability of Stem Cells in the United States," Cold Spring Harbor Laboratory Press, December 2015, https://www.ncbi.nlm.nih.gov/pmc/articles/PMC4665039.

20. Jane E. Brody, "Do Egg Donors Face Long-Term Risks?" July 10, 2017, https://www.nytimes.com/2017/07/10/well/live/are-there-long-term-risks-to-egg-donors.html.

21. Kevin Loria, "Designer babies are coming—here's why some think that's a good thing," August 4, 2015, https://www.businessinsider.com/why-we-should-allow-designer-babies-2015-8.

22. Jewels Green, "Test-tube babies are all grown up . . . and they're not happy," July 6, 2016, https://anonymousus.org/filling-out-the-story/, https://www.lifesitenews.com/news/test-tube-babies-are-all-grown-up...and-theyre-not-happy.

23. Pia Peterson, "He Found Out He Had 32 Siblings. For The Times Magazine, He Took Their Pictures," *Times Insider*, June 29, 2019, https://www.nytimes.com/interactive/2019/06/26/magazine/sperm-donor-siblings.html.

24. Brody, "Do Egg Donors Face Long-Term Risks?"

25. K. Blaine, "The Dangerous Effects of Surrogacy: A Review of *A Transnational Feminist View of Surrogacy Biomarkets in India*," October 29, 2018, the Witherspoon Institute, https://www.thepublicdiscourse.com/2018/10/42720/.

26. Rachel Lu, "No to the Baby Market," September 12, 2016, https://www.nationalreview.com/2016/09/surrogacy-ethics-assisted-reproductive-technology-baby-market/?itm_source=parsely-api.

27. Kathryn Jean Lopez, "The Pro-Life Movement Shouldn't Embrace Surrogacy," interview, December 9, 2017, https://www.nationalreview.com/2017/12/surrogacy-not-truly-pro-life/

28. Lu, "No to the Baby Market."

29. Lopez, "The Pro-Life Movement Shouldn't Embrace Surrogacy."

30. Lu, "No to the Baby Market."

31. Creighton Model Fertility*Care* System, FertilityCare Services of Venice, http://www.fertilitycarevenice.org/naprotechnology-vs-ivf.

32. Ibid.

Chapter 12

1. Carrie Mumah, "Planned Parenthood of Greater New York Announces Intent to Remove Margaret Sanger's Name from NYC Health Center," July 21, 2020, https://www.plannedparenthood.org/planned-parenthood-greater-new-york/about/news/planned-parenthood-of-greater-new-york-announces-intent-to-remove-margaret-sangers-name-from-nyc-health-center.

2. Anne Barbeau Gardiner, *Margaret Sanger's Multifaceted Defense of Abortion and Infanticide*, University Faculty for Life, http://www.uffl.org/vol16/gardiner06.pdf.

3. Willis L. Krumholz, "Yes, Planned Parenthood Targets And Hurts Poor Black Women," February 18, 2016, https://thefederalist.com/2016/02/18/yes-planned-parenthood-targets-and-hurts-poor-black-women/.

4. Steven Ertelt, "Poll: 55% of Americans Don't Know Planned Parenthood Does Abortions," April 29, 2013, https://www.lifenews.com/2013/04/29/poll-55-of-americans-dont-know-planned-parenthood-does-abortions/.

5. Ibid.

6. Dave Umhoefer, "Glenn Grothman says Planned Parenthood is leading abortion provider," the Poynter Institute, May 15, 2017, https://www.politifact.com/factchecks/2017/may/15/glenn-grothman/glenn-grothman-says-planned-parenthood-leading-abo/.

7. Annual Report, 2018–19, Planned Parenthood, https://www.plannedparenthood.org/uploads/filer_public/2e/da/2eda3f50-82aa-4ddb-acce-c2854c4ea80b/2018-2019_annual_report.pdf

8. Kenneth D. Kochanek, MA, Jiaquan Xu, MD, and Elizabeth Arias, PhD, "Mortality in the United States, 2019," Data Brief 395, December 2020, National Center for Health Statistics, https://www.cdc.gov/nchs/fastats/leading-causes-of-death.htm.

9. Emily Ward, "Report: Planned Parenthood Operates Over Half of U.S. Abortion Clinics," February 15, 2019, https://www.cnsnews.com/news/article/emily-ward/report-planned-parenthood-operates-over-half-us-abortion-clinics.

10. Erin Schumaker, "Clinics where majority of US patients get abortions are rapidly closing: Report," December 11, 2019, https://abcnews.go.com/Health/clinics-majority-women-abortions-rapidly-closing-report/story?id=67624226.

11. Wm. Robert Johnston, "Historical abortion statistics, United States," January 14, 2020, http://www.johnstonsarchive.net/policy/abortion/ab-unitedstates.html.

12. Melanie Israel, "Planned Parenthood by the Numbers," the Heritage Foundation, April 6, 2020, https://www.heritage.org/life/report/planned-parenthood-the-numbers.

13. Annual Report, 2018–19, Planned Parenthood.

14. https://www.plannedparenthood.org/learn/abortion/the-abortion-pill/how-do-i-get-the-abortion-pill

15. Annual Report, 2018–19, Planned Parenthood.

16. Ibid.

17. Abby Johnson, "Exposing the Planned Parenthood business model," April 4, 2011, https://thehill.com/blogs/congress-blog/politics/153699-exposing-the-planned-parenthood-business-model.

18. Ibid.

19. Leana Wen (@DrLeanaWen), Twitter, January 8, 2019, https://twitter.com/DrLeanaWen/status/1082660986513960966.

20. Colin Campbell, "Former Baltimore health commissioner Leana Wen, Planned Parenthood resolve dispute over severance, benefits,"

September 18, 2019, https://www.baltimoresun.com/politics/bs-md-pol-wen-planned-parenthood-folo-20190917-5pflyoimfzgmphhqi7t3xj2uhu-story.html.

21. D'Angelo Gore, "Planned Parenthood's Services," September 4, 2015, https://www.factcheck.org/2015/09/planned-parenthoods-services/.

22. Annual Report, 2019–20, Planned Parenthood, https://www.plannedparenthood.org/uploads/filer_public/67/30/67305ea1-8da2-4cee-9191-19228c1d6f70/210219-annual-report-2019-2020-web-final.pdf.

23. Staff, "Explanation of Planned Parenthood Alternatives," April 4, 0217, Concerned Women for America Legislative Action Committee, https://concernedwomen.org/explanation-of-planned-parenthood-alternatives/.

24. Matt Hadro, "Does defunding Planned Parenthood really threaten women's health?" January 18, 2017, https://www.catholicnewsagency.com/news/35257/does-defunding-planned-parenthood-really-threaten-womens-health.

25. Michelle Ye Hee Lee, "The repeated, misleading claim that Planned Parenthood 'provides' mammograms," October 2, 2015, https://www.washingtonpost.com/news/fact-checker/wp/2015/10/02/the-repeated-misleading-claim-that-planned-parenthood-provides-mammograms/.

26. Marguerite Duane and Charles Donovan, "The facts about healthcare alternatives to Planned Parenthood," May 20, 2017, https://www.washingtonexaminer.com/the-facts-about-healthcare-alternatives-to-planned-parenthood.

27. Charles A. "Chuck" Donovan and James Studnicki, "Planned Parenthood: 'Irreplaceable' and 'Lifesaving'?" Charlotte Lozier Institute, August 2, 2017, https://lozierinstitute.org/planned-parenthood-irreplaceable-and-lifesaving/.

28. Lila Rose, "The Numbers That Show Planned Parenthood About Abortion, Not Women's Health," September 14, 2016, https://www.dailysignal.com/2016/09/14/the-numbers-that-show-planned-parenthood-about-abortion-not-womens-health/.

29. Donovan and Studnicki, "Planned Parenthood: 'Irreplaceable' and 'Lifesaving'?"

30. Israel, "Planned Parenthood by the Numbers," Backgrounder 3472.

31. Donovan and Studnicki, "Planned Parenthood: 'Irreplaceable' and 'Lifesaving'?"

32. Kristi Keck, "Big Tobacco: A history of its decline," June 19, 2009, https://edition.cnn.com/2009/POLITICS/06/19/tobacco.decline/.

33. Michael S Givel and Stanton A Glantz, "Tobacco lobby political influence on US state legislatures in the 1990s," *Tobacco Control* 10:2 (2001), https://tobaccocontrol.bmj.com/content/10/2/124.full.

34. Keck, "Big Tobacco: A history of its decline."

35. David Heath, "Contesting the Science of Smoking," May 4, 2016, https://www.theatlantic.com/politics/archive/2016/05/low-tar-cigarettes/481116/.

36. Keck, "Big Tobacco: A history of its decline."

37. Heath, "Contesting the Science of Smoking."

38. Annual Report, 2019–2020, Planned Parenthood.

39. https://www.plannedparenthood.org/about-us/who-we-are/our-history

40. https://www.plannedparenthoodaction.org/about-us

41. Zack Budryk, "Planned Parenthood launches $45M campaign to back Democrats in 2020," January 16, 2020, https://thehill.com/policy/healthcare/abortion/478548-planned-parenthood-launches-45m-campaign-to-support-democrats-in.

42. "Illinois Abortion Law Guide: What does the Reproductive Health Act mean?" June 14, 2019, https://abc7chicago.com/illinois-abortion-law-in-laws/5345982/.

43. Anna North, "While some states try to ban abortion, these states are expanding access," June 20, 2019, https://www.vox.com/identities/2019/6/12/18662738/abortion-bill-illinois-maine-laws-new-york.

44. Ibid.

45. Anna North, "Nevada is lifting abortion restrictions, even as other states pass near-total bans," May 22, 2019, https://www.vox.com/2019/5/22/18635687/trust-nevada-women-act-abortion-laws-2019.

46. "Emotional and Mental Health After Abortion," Guttmacher Institute, https://www.guttmacher.org/perspectives50/emotional-and-mental-health-after-abortion.

47. "Abortion and Mental Health Risks," the Elliot Institute, https://afterabortion.org/abortion-risks-a-list-of-major-psychological-complications-related-to-abortion/.

Chapter 13

1. Margaret Sanger, "High Lights in the History of Birth Control," the *Thinker*, October 1923, https://www.nyu.edu/projects/sanger/webedition/app/documents/show.php?sangerDoc=306641.xml.

2. Angela Watson, "You can do anything, but you can't do everything" (blog), the Cornerstone for Teachers, https://thecornerstoneforteachers.com/you-can-do-anything-but-you-cant-do-everything/.

3. Gilda Sedgh, ScD, et al., "Abortion incidence between 1990 and 2014: global, regional, and subregional levels and trends," National Center for Biotechnology Information, May 11, 2016, https://www.ncbi.nlm.nih.gov/pmc/articles/PMC5498988/.

4. "The top 10 causes of death," World Health Organization, December 9, 2020, https://www.who.int/news-room/fact-sheets/detail/the-top-10-causes-of-death.

5. Kenneth D. Kochanek, MA, Jiaquan Xu, MD, and Elizabeth Arias, PhD, "Mortality in the United States, 2019," Data Brief 395, December 2020, National Center for Health Statistics, https://www.cdc.gov/nchs/fastats/leading-causes-of-death.htm.

6. Elizabeth Nash and Joerg Dreweke, "The U.S. Abortion Rate Continues to Drop: Once Again, State Abortion Restrictions Are Not the Main Driver," September 18, 2019, Guttmacher Institute, https://www.guttmacher.org/gpr/2019/09/us-abortion-rate-continues-drop-once-again-state-abortion-restrictions-are-not-main.

7. Adam Wagner, "How the Holocaust impacted human rights," the *Jewish Chronicle*, January 27, 2019, https://www.thejc.com/comment/opinion/adam-wagner-how-the-holocaust-impacted-human-rights-1.479104.

8. Joshua Barajas, "How the Nazi's defense of 'just following orders' plays out in the mind," February 20, 2016, https://www.pbs.org/newshour/science/how-the-nazis-defense-of-just-following-orders-plays-out-in-the-mind.

9. Wagner, "How the Holocaust impacted human rights."

10. https://www.nuernberg.de/internet/menschenrechte_e/im_wortlaut_e.html

Conclusion

1. "A saintly woman," *John Harvard's Journal*, July–August 1982, https://harvardmagazine.com/sites/default/files/mother_teresa-class-day-82.pdf.

About the Authors

Shawn Carney (left) is the cofounder, CEO, and president of 40 Days for Life and one of the most sought-after pro-life speakers today. He began as a volunteer in the pro-life movement while still in college. During this time, he helped to lead the first-ever local 40 Days for Life campaign before helping launch it to now 950 cities in 65 countries.

In 2019, Shawn and his wife, Marilisa, were portrayed in the major motion picture *Unplanned* for their role in helping former Planned Parenthood director Abby Johnson during her conversion. Abby was number 26 out of more than 200 abortion workers to date who have reached out to 40 Days for Life.

Shawn is a regular media spokesperson, and his work has been featured on hundreds of outlets—including NBC News, Fox News, Fox & Friends, the Glenn Beck Show, the Laura

Ingraham Show, BBC, *The Guardian*, *USA Today*—and Christian media—including *The Christian Post*, *National Catholic Register*, Sirius XM Catholic Radio, EWTN Radio, and Focus on the Family.

Shawn has addressed audiences coast to coast and internationally. He has executive produced and hosted award-winning pro-life documentaries and is the host of the weekly *40 Days for Life Podcast*. Shawn is the coauthor of *40 Days for Life* and the author of the national best-sellers *The Beginning of the End of Abortion* and *To the Heart of the Matter*. He is a member of the Knights of Columbus and the Equestrian Order of the Holy Sepulcher of Jerusalem. Shawn lives in Texas with Marilisa and their eight children.

Steve Karlen is the campaign director at 40 Days for Life. After Steve helped lead a statewide coalition that prevented the University of Wisconsin Hospital and Clinics from opening a late-term abortion facility near the campus of his alma mater, Steve was asked to serve on the 40 Days for Life headquarters team. In this role, Steve has helped spread the 40 Days for Life mission across the United States, Canada, and Mexico.

Steve is the editor of *Day 41* magazine and the cohost of the *40 Days for Life Podcast*. He is the author of the book *This Is When We Begin to Fight* and has spoken in all fifty states, four Canadian provinces, and Mexico City. Steve and his work have been featured on American Family Radio, EWTN, the Christian Broadcasting Network, and NBC, CBS, and Fox affiliates as well as numerous newspapers and radio stations.

Steve lives in Madison, Wisconsin, with his wife, Laura, and their five children.

40 DAYS FOR LIFE.

Now that you know what to say when . . . be part of the beginning of the end of abortion!

PRAY MORE!

Find your closest 40 Days for Life vigil today:

40daysforlife.com/locations

READ MORE!

Keep up with saved lives, abortion worker conversions, and the pulse of the pro-life movement by receiving *DAY 41* quarterly magazine for FREE! Sign up at

40daysforlife.com/magazine

LISTEN MORE!

Download the weekly *40 Days for Life Podcast* for free. Guests include Peter Kreeft, Eric Metaxas, Alan Keyes, Father Paul Scalia, Benjamin Watson, Lila Rose, former abortion workers, and many more. Listen on any podcast app, the 40 Days for Life app, or at

40daysforlife.com/podcast

At **40daysforlifegear.com**, get exclusive discounts on signed copies of this book and the national best sellers written by Shawn Carney, including *The Beginning of the End of Abortion* and *To the Heart of the Matter*, and Steve Karlen's *This Is When We Begin to Fight*.

Invite Shawn Carney or Steve Karlen to speak at your event by emailing **media@40daysforlife.com**.

Find out more at 40daysforlife.com